COACHING
4-3-3 TACTICS

154 TACTICAL SOLUTIONS & PRACTICES

WRITTEN BY

MASSIMO LUCCHESI

PUBLISHED BY

COACHING
4-3-3 TACTICS

154 TACTICAL SOLUTIONS & PRACTICES

First Published January 2019 by SoccerTutor.com

Info@soccertutor.com | www.SoccerTutor.com

UK: 0208 1234 007 | **US:** (305) 767 4443 | **ROTW:** +44 208 1234 007

ISBN: 978-1-910491-26-3

Author

Massimo Lucchesi

Edited by

Alex Fitzgerald - SoccerTutor.com

Cover Design by

Alex Macrides, Think Out Of The Box Ltd.
Email: design@thinkootb.com Tel: +44 (0) 208 144 3550

Diagrams

Diagram designs by SoccerTutor.com. All the diagrams in this book have been created using SoccerTutor.com Tactics Manager Software available from *www.SoccerTutor.com*

Note: While every effort has been made to ensure the technical accuracy of the content of this book, neither the author nor publishers can accept any responsibility for any injury or loss sustained as a result of the use of this material.

CONTENTS

COACH PROFILE: MASSIMO LUCCHESI

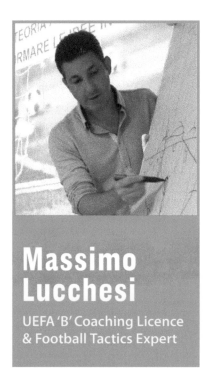

Massimo Lucchesi

UEFA 'B' Coaching Licence
& Football Tactics Expert

- **Director of Allenatore.net** - Italy's #1 football coaching publisher and digital platform

- **Author of 17 top selling football coaching books** in English, German, Greek and Russian language

- **Winner of the Italian FA (FIGC) Award for "Best Coaching Book" 2018** ('Liquid Organisation,' 2018 Allenatore.net)

- **Football Tactics Expert:**

  » Massimo Lucchesi is a football tactics expert and has conducted over 100 seminars across the world in Italy, USA, Russia, Greece, Mexico, Romania, Jamaica, Cyprus and Slovakia.

  » Massimo never stops learning and is always looking to learn more by observing the training sessions of the best coaches in the world, such as Carlo Ancelotti, Luis Enrique, Antonio Conte, Pep Guardiola, Maurizio Sarri, Diego Simeone + many more...

  » Massimo has also had the opportunity to visit some of the best academies in Europe, such as Barcelona, Benfica, Anderlecht and Schalke, to learn the best strategies to develop young players.

INTRODUCTION

A well-organised team, in which all players know how to recognise different tactical situations and support each other, is able to enhance the characteristics of the individual and allow them to produce higher quality performances.

All of this can of course have a big impact on the results of the team and the progress in the season.

On the other hand, a team is unlikely to be able to express itself consistently and achieve satisfactory results, even if they are made up of technically skilled players, if the players are not able to communicate with each other and interact effectively.

This brief but important premise shows how important the organisation of the game is.

The aim of the book is to highlight the principles that coaches must know and use to organise the modern game system, which is no longer a rigid entity and that inhibits the expression and growth of the individual through a mechanical execution - it is now a flexible environment where players know how to recognise tactical processes and relate to each other within shapes and geometric structures, to solve specific tactical situations within different areas of the pitch.

I wish you good reading and good work!

MASSIMO LUCCHESI

TACTICAL STRUCTURE OF THE 4-3-3 FORMATION

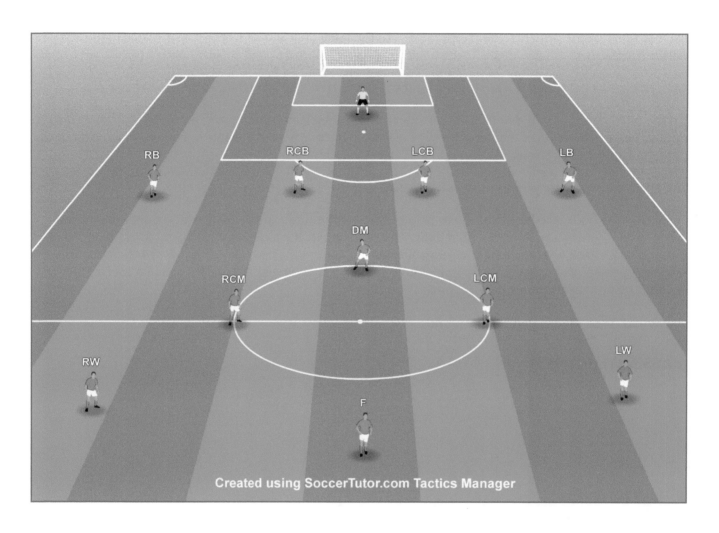

Created using SoccerTutor.com Tactics Manager

- **RB:** Right Back
- **LB:** Left Back
- **RCB:** Right Centre Back
- **LCB:** Left Centre Back
- **DM:** Defensive Midfielder

- **RCM:** Right Central Midfielder
- **LCM:** Left Central Midfielder
- **RW:** Right Winger
- **LW:** Left Winger
- **F:** Forward

DIAGRAM KEY

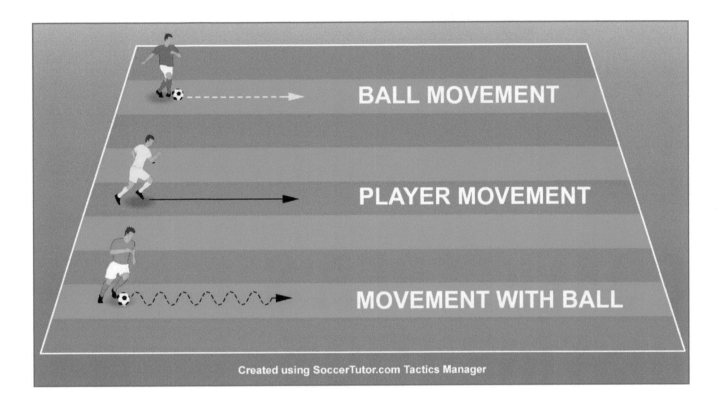

PRACTICE FORMAT

Each practice includes clear diagrams with supporting training notes such as:

- Name of Practice

- Objective of Practice

- Practice Description

- Progressions/Coaching Points if applicable

CHAPTER I

GOALKEEPER'S DISTRIBUTION FROM GOAL KICKS

GOALKEEPER'S DISTRIBUTION FROM GOAL KICKS

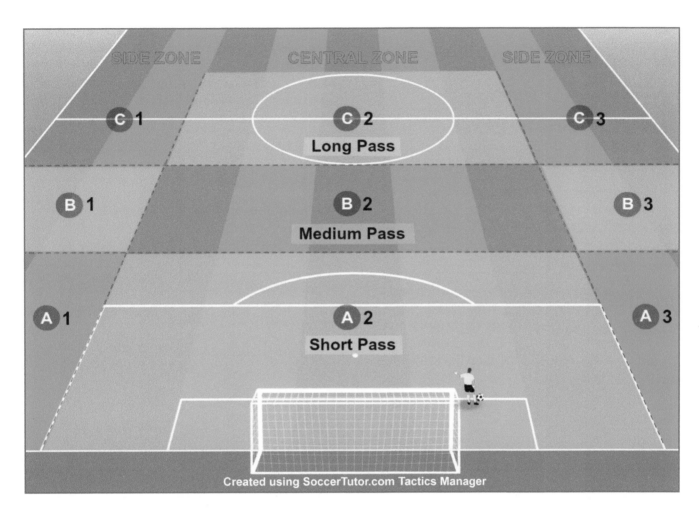

The goalkeeper is directly involved in the build up/ attacking phase in the following situations:

1. **Goal kicks**
2. **After catching the ball with the hands**
3. **After receiving a back pass from a teammate**

The goalkeeper's role requires him to quickly make the best choice in the specific game situation. Depending on the tactical organisation of the opposition, the goalkeeper will choose one of the following options from a goal kick:

1. **Short Pass**
2. **Medium Pass**
3. **Long Pass** (in the direction of a player who is good in the air)

In addition, the goalkeeper can decide whether to play toward the flanks (side zones) or toward the central zones of the pitch.

By dividing the pitch into horizontal and vertical sections, we identify 9 different zones that provide all the options for the goalkeeper when taking a goal kick (**see diagram above**).

TACTICAL SOLUTIONS FOR DISTRIBUTION FROM GOAL KICKS AGAINST DIFFERENT FORMATIONS

POSITIONING OF ATTACKING PLAYERS

The first thing to consider is how many players to position past the halfway line.

This way, the opposition will have to decide whether they accept a situation of equal numbers in their defensive zone, or if they prefer to have an extra player to ensure a numerical advantage.

If the opposition contests our attackers with the same number of players (e.g. 3 v 3), it is advantageous to use a long goal kick. The goalkeeper would aim for Zone C2 (see previous page) and we would push our midfielders close to our 3 forwards.

If, instead, as most often happens, the opposition prefer to have an extra player in their back line (e.g. 4 v 3), it is then better to "isolate" the opposition's defensive unit from their midfield and attacking players by using a short or medium goal kick - **see diagram below**.

SHORT GOAL KICK

When using a short goal kick, it is important to push our centre backs toward the flanks, outside of the penalty box. Their actual distance from the sideline depends on the positioning of the opposition's midfielders and forwards.

It is very important to verify this situation to make sure that our goalkeeper can make a successful short pass, which helps us build up play.

If this is not the case, as often happens in modern football, it's important to do a quick tactical analysis regarding the positioning of the opponents and then adjust accordingly.

On the following pages, we display many different options for the goalkeeper's distribution from goal kicks against different attacking formations.

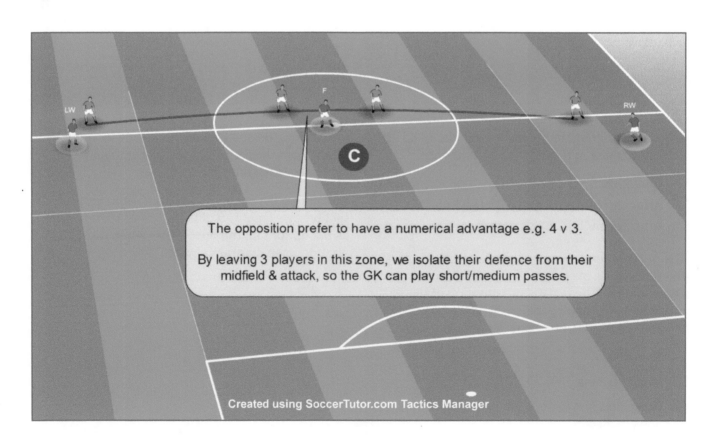

The opposition prefer to have a numerical advantage e.g. 4 v 3.

By leaving 3 players in this zone, we isolate their defence from their midfield & attack, so the GK can play short/medium passes.

Created using SoccerTutor.com Tactics Manager

Goal Kicks Against Opponents in a 5-1 Attacking Formation

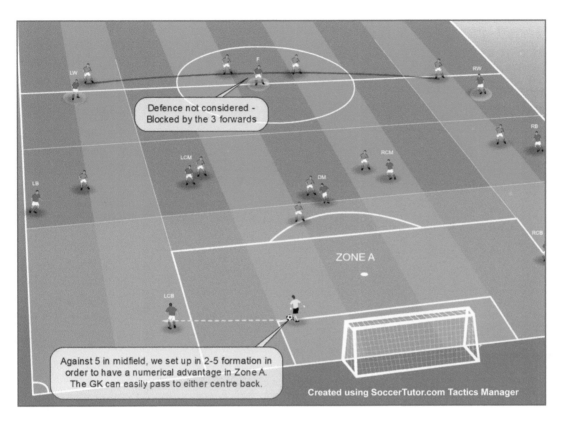

When the opposition are in a 5-1 formation, we don't consider their defensive players because they are "blocked" by our 3 forwards.

We position our defence and midfield into a 2-5 formation, in order to have a numerical advantage in zone A and start with a short pass. The goalkeeper can easily pass to either centre back.

Goal Kicks Against Opponents in a 4-2 Attacking Formation

When the opposition are in a 4-2 formation, we position our defence and midfield into a 3-4 formation, in order to have a numerical advantage in zone A and start with a short pass.

The goalkeeper can pass to the defensive midfielder, who is the spare man in space to receive.

Goal Kicks Against Opponents in a 3-3 Attacking Formation

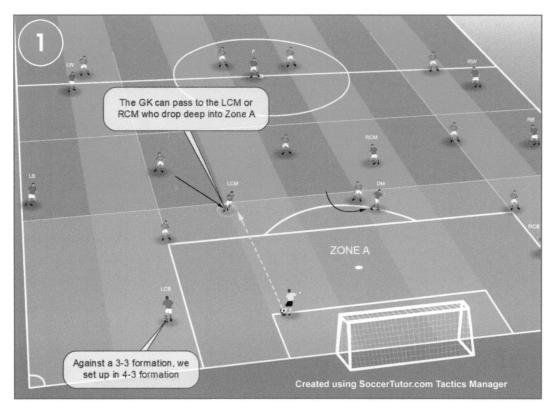

The GK can pass to the LCM or RCM who drop deep into Zone A

ZONE A

Against a 3-3 formation, we set up in 4-3 formation

Created using SoccerTutor.com Tactics Manager

When the opposition are in a 3-3 formation, we position our defence and midfield into a 4-3 formation, in order to have a numerical advantage in zone A and start with a short pass.

The goalkeeper can pass to the LCM or RCM who drop off into Zone A to receive in space.

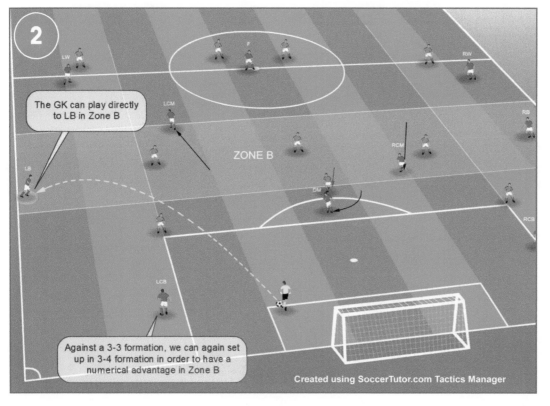

The GK can play directly to LB in Zone B

ZONE B

Against a 3-3 formation, we can again set up in 3-4 formation in order to have a numerical advantage in Zone B

Created using SoccerTutor.com Tactics Manager

When the opposition are in a 3-3 formation, we can also position our defence and midfield into a 3-4 formation, in order to have a numerical advantage in Zone B and utilise a medium length pass to distribute to the full backs near the sidelines.

In this example, the goalkeeper passes to the left back.

If the passes from the 2 previous examples are not available due to intelligent positioning and good tracking of movement from our opponents, then the goalkeeper can play a long pass into Zone C towards the wingers who are in 1 v 1 situations.

It is best to pass to the winger with the best heading ability.

Goal Kicks Against Opponents in a 2-4 Attacking Formation

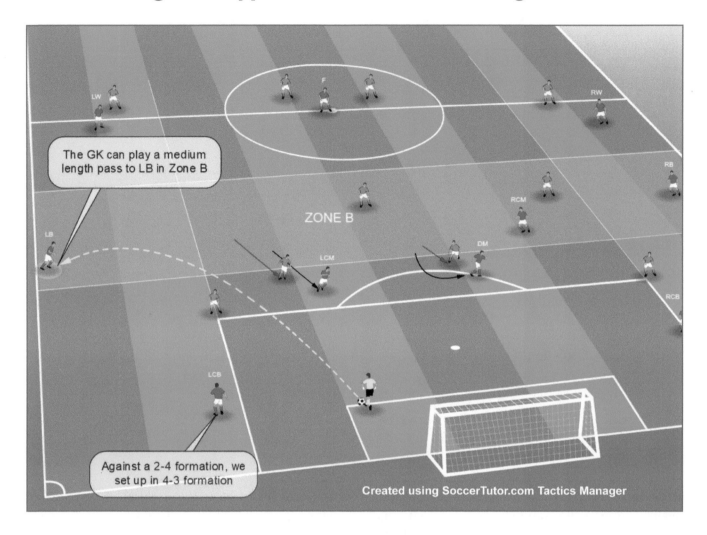

The GK can play a medium length pass to LB in Zone B

ZONE B

Against a 2-4 formation, we set up in 4-3 formation

Created using SoccerTutor.com Tactics Manager

When the opposition are in a 2-4 formation, we position our defence and midfield into a 4-3 formation.

Our back 4 and central midfielders are most often marked. This leaves one of the full backs free in Zone B.

The goalkeeper can play a medium length pass to a full back free in space.

CHAPTER 2

BUILD UP PLAY TO COUNTERACT DIFFERENT TYPES OF PRESSING

THE DIFFERENT TYPES OF BUILD UP PLAY

The build up phase has 3 fundamental types:

1. MANOVRATA: Build Up Play Against Teams that Only Press with their Forwards

Opponents who decide not to press high as a team encourage us to play the ball forward and advance up the pitch. In this tactical situation, the first objective is to overcome the opposition's attacking players. After this is achieved, we work on developing the "Creating Phase," which we will analyse later.

2. ACCELERATA: Build Up Play Against Teams that Press with their Forwards & Midfield (No Space in Behind)

This describes when the opposition use aggressive pressing high up the pitch with their attackers and midfielders, but their defenders keep a relatively deep defensive line to stop the ball being played easily in behind with long passes.

In this situation, the pressing of the opponent's attacking group can be bypassed by directing passes in behind their midfield line, most often to the winger who moves inside off the flank. We take advantage of the conservative approach of the opponent's defensive line, which doesn't move up too much as they are wary of providing depth to our attacking players.

3. DIRETTA: Direct Build Up Play Against Teams that Press with their Full Team (Space in Behind)

"Direct Build Up" is used when the opposition is very aggressive, to the extent of even having their defensive players support the pressing of the rest of our team. In this situation, the opposing defenders try to anticipate when the ball will be directed to our forwards. The most appropriate play in these situations is to use long passes in behind the defensive line, to fully exploit the space in the opposition's half.

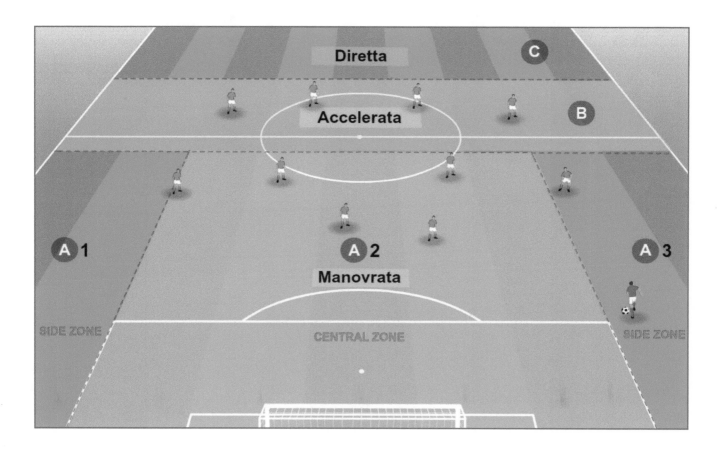

I. BUILD UP PLAY AGAINST TEAMS THAT ONLY PRESS WITH THEIR FORWARDS

1.1 - CREATING A NUMERICAL ADVANTAGE AT THE BACK TO MOVE THE BALL TO THE FREE PLAYER

When building up play against teams that only press with their forwards, our goalkeeper has started with a short pass and the organisation of the opposition (only forwards pressing) encourages us to advance with the ball. In these situations, it is important to have a clear tactical reading of the game, in order to create a numerical advantage by shifting the marking of our opponents. To help the reading of the game, it's important to identify the positioning of the opposing players and divide the pitch into zones and sectors (**please see diagram below**).

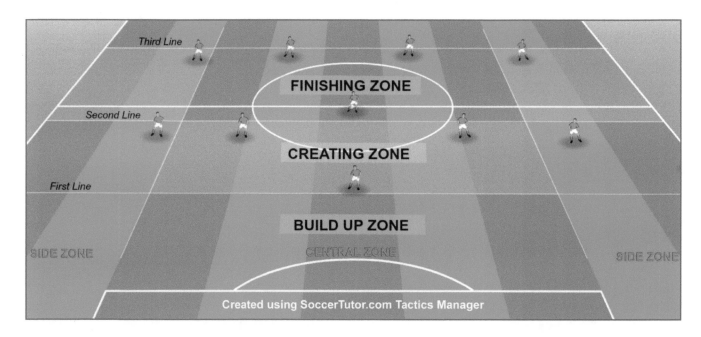

Created using SoccerTutor.com Tactics Manager

Without taking the opposition's 4 defenders into consideration (because our 3 attackers keep them occupied), the rest of the opposing players generally form one of these tactical formations: 4-2 (or 4-1-1), 5-1 (or 1-4-1) and 3-3 (or 3-1-2).

For each of these possible formations, we have 3 different build up tactics to "eliminate" the opponent and advance up the pitch.

This can be done by:

- 1.1 - **Creating a Numerical Advantage at the Back to Move the Ball to the Free Player**

- 1.2 - **Direct Pass into Midfield**

- 1.3 - **Indirect Pass into Midfield Using a "Link Player"**

These are our aims for playing the ball to the free player who can receive and move forward:

1. Create a numerical advantage at the back to overcome the pressing of the opposing forwards using horizontal passes to switch play from one side to the other quickly (this can involve the goalkeeper).

2. Advance with the ball once overcoming the opposing forwards and pass to a close teammate that has freed himself from marking. This player can then use the space to move forward.

3. Execute the processes for build up play in a safe way, through intelligent compensating movements.

Now we follow with some examples to demonstrate how to create and take advantage of a numerical advantage at the back when the opposition only initially press with their forwards.

Defensive Midfielder Drops into the Centre of Defence vs 4-4-2

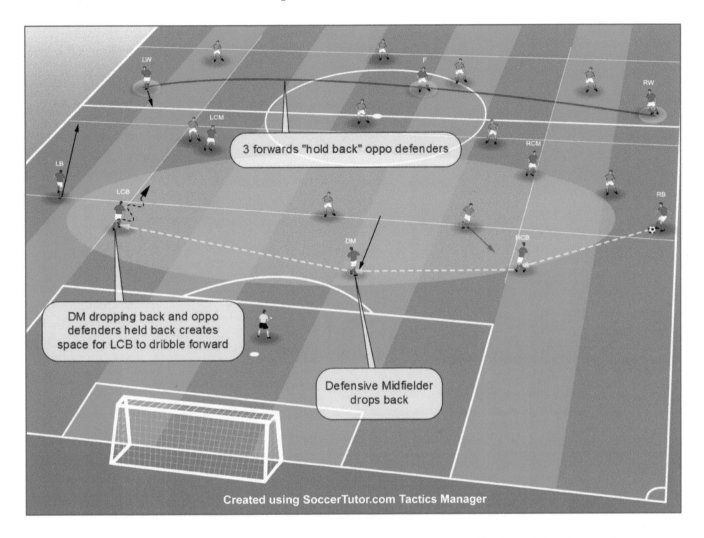

In this example against the 4-4-2, the defensive midfielder (DM) drops back into the middle of the defensive line.

This expands the width of the back line, giving the opportunity for one of our centre backs (LCB in diagram) to receive in space and dribble the ball forward.

For this to work, it is of fundamental importance that our 3 attackers (wingers and forward) "hold back" the opposing 4 defenders and keep them occupied. This way, we create the space for our build up to be successful.

At the same time, all of our defenders and midfielders have to be constantly alert and involved, keeping in mind the option of passing back to our goalkeeper to restart the build up process, if necessary.

Central Midfielder Drops Back to Receive vs 4-4-2

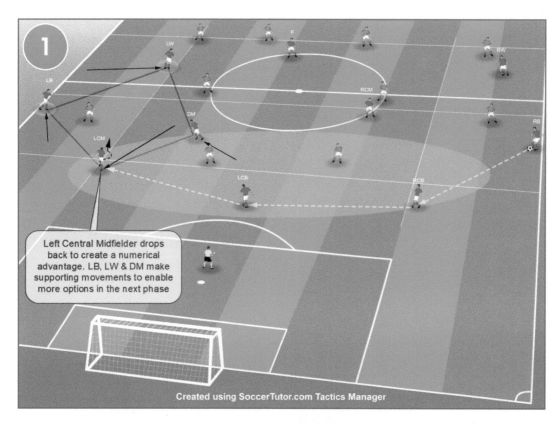

Left Central Midfielder drops back to create a numerical advantage. LB, LW & DM make supporting movements to enable more options in the next phase

Created using SoccerTutor.com Tactics Manager

In this second example, it is one of the central midfielders (LCM in the diagram example) dropping back and creating a numerical advantage in the back line.

The left back (LB) and the left winger (LW) make movements to create a rhombus shape, which enables more options for the next phase to follow.

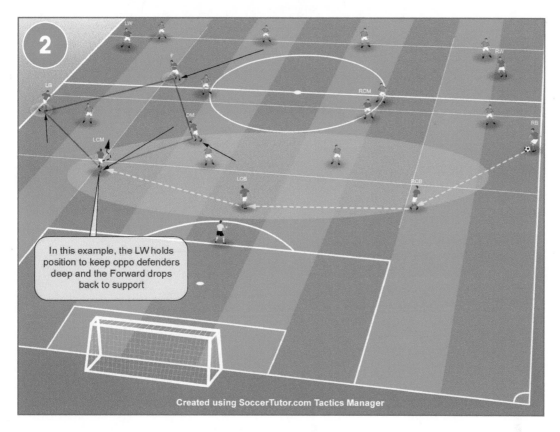

In this example, the LW holds position to keep oppo defenders deep and the Forward drops back to support

Created using SoccerTutor.com Tactics Manager

In this variation of the central midfielder dropping back and dribbling forward, different players cooperate in creating the rhombus shape.

It is now the forward (F) at the top of the rhombus as he drops back, while the left winger (LW) remains wide to keep the opposing right back in a deep position.

Exploiting 2 v 1 Numerical Advantage at the Back Against 1 Forward with Our Central Midfielder at Top of the Rhombus

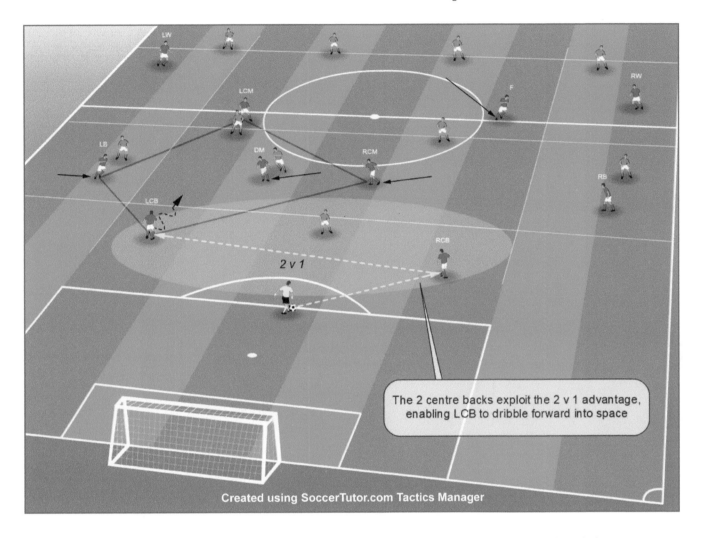

The 2 centre backs exploit the 2 v 1 advantage, enabling LCB to dribble forward into space

Created using SoccerTutor.com Tactics Manager

This diagram shows the opposing team with 1 forward and a No.10 (or second/withdrawn forward), who marks our defensive midfielder. The opposition could be using the 4-4-1-1, 4-5-1 or 4-2-3-1.

As the opposition's No.10 (or second/withdrawn forward) is marking our defensive midfielder, we can then exploit the 2 v 1 numerical advantage that our centre backs have.

Due to the 2 v 1 advantage, one of our centre backs can easily receive in space and dribble the ball forward (LCB in diagram example).

At the same time, the left back (LB) and the left central midfielder (LCM) both move to form a rhombus shape (see blue lines in diagram), which will help the centre back in possession advance the attacking move with several available options.

If the opposing No.10 (or second/withdrawn forward) moves forward to mark our defensive midfielder tightly, as is likely to happen, the defensive midfielder will move away to take his marker with him, thus allowing the right central midfielder (RCM) to be part of the rhombus, and in a very good position to receive the ball.

If after playing his pass, the left centre back (LCB) receives the ball back, he can then pass to the right centre back (RCB). When he receives in space, the forward then becomes the top of the new rhombus shape formed on the right side, while the wingers (LW and RW) stay wide and high up so the team are open and spread out, using the full space.

Exploiting 2 v 1 Numerical Advantage at the Back Against 1 Forward with Our Forward at Top of the Rhombus

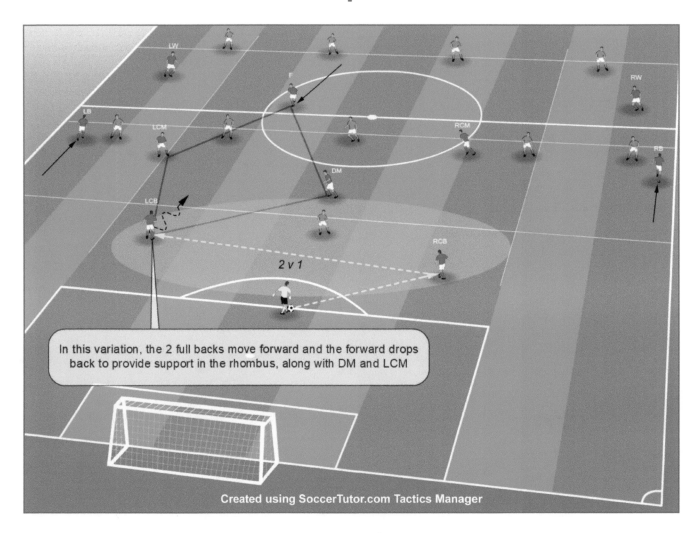

In this variation, the 2 full backs move forward and the forward drops back to provide support in the rhombus, along with DM and LCM

Created using SoccerTutor.com Tactics Manager

In this diagram, we show a variation of the previous example.

This time, when the left centre back (LCB) receives, the left back moves forward, rather than inside. The forward drops back to position himself at the top of the rhombus. The left central midfielder (LCM) and the defensive midfielder (DM) provide the side support for the rhombus shape.

The centre back can again move forward and has many options to progress the attack.

However, even in this situation, further development of the attacking play depends on the opponent's approach and the reactions of their players.

How to Build Up Play Against 2 Forwards and a No.10

We have examined how to create and exploit a numerical advantage at the back against 2 forwards and against 1 forward and a No.10 (or second/ withdrawn forward). Let's now discuss options to overcome an opposition with 2 forwards and a No.10.

In these situations, we must take advantage of the freedom initially allowed to the full back. We can then move our midfielders and forwards to that side of the pitch, as shown in the 2 diagrams to follow.

The objective is to quickly create a rhombus shape (see blue lines in next 2 diagrams) to provide plenty of options for the full back in possession.

OPTION 1: Central Midfielder Moves Wide & the Winger Moves to Top of Rhombus

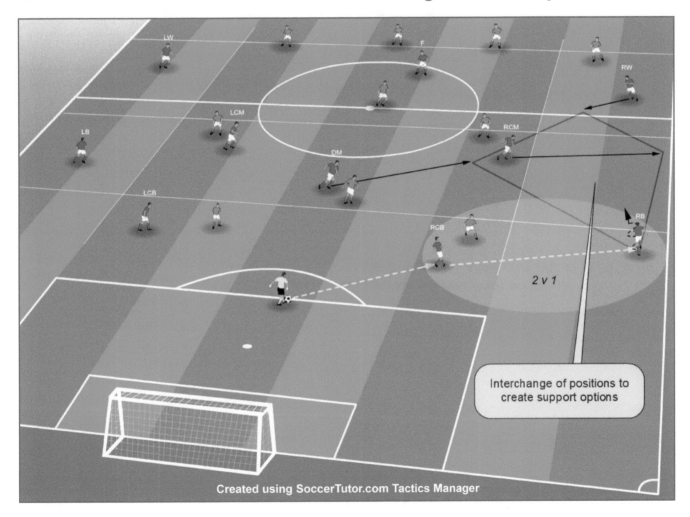

In this first example, the central midfielder (RCM) moves wide to function as wide support, with the right winger (RW) functioning as the support at the top of the rhombus.

OPTION 2: Winger Provides Wide Support & the Forward Moves to Top of Rhombus

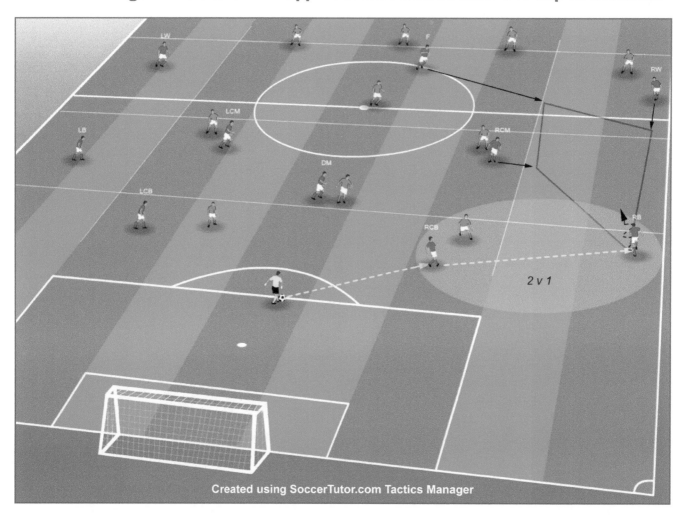

Created using SoccerTutor.com Tactics Manager

In this second example, the right winger (RW) drops back to provide wide support and the forward (F) moves across to function as the support at the top of the rhombus.

I.2 - DIRECT PASS INTO MIDFIELD

It is not always necessary to dribble the ball forward to get through (bypass) the line of the opposing forwards.

In some situations, it is convenient to pass into midfield (directly or indirectly). If there is a teammate free of marking and in space to receive a pass, he should be able to turn and proceed with the attack.

With the 4-3-3 formation, the ideal player to receive this pass from one of the defenders into midfield is the defensive midfielder (DM), especially when we face a team playing with 2 forwards.

The diagram below clearly shows how to exploit this match up in the middle of the pitch.

Centre Back Passes into the Centre to the Defensive Midfielder

To quickly advance forward with many options, the centre back's (RCB) best option in this example is to pass to the DM in between the 2 forwards

Created using SoccerTutor.com Tactics Manager

The opposition are using the 4-4-2 formation with 2 forwards up against our 2 centre backs.

Our 2 full backs and 2 central midfielders (LCM and RCM) are then occupied by the opposing team's 4 midfielders. This leaves our defensive midfielder (DM) free in space to receive.

In this diagram example, the right centre back's best option is to pass in between the 2 opposing forwards to the defensive midfielder. The defensive midfielder can turn and move forward with the ball. Our team can therefore advance the attack with many different options.

1.3 - INDIRECT PASS INTO MIDFIELD USING A "LINK PLAYER"

We have to recognise that a tactically well organised opponent will try to counter the "easy" tactic that we displayed on the previous page. Therefore, we have to be ready with counter adjustments, in order to eliminate the pressure from our opponents and successfully progress our attacking play.

The diagram below shows how to get around the pressing of our centre back and play the ball to our defensive midfielder (DM) via a one touch pass from a central midfielder (RCM in diagram example).

Using a "Link Player" to Get Around the Pressing of Our Centre Back Against 2 Forwards

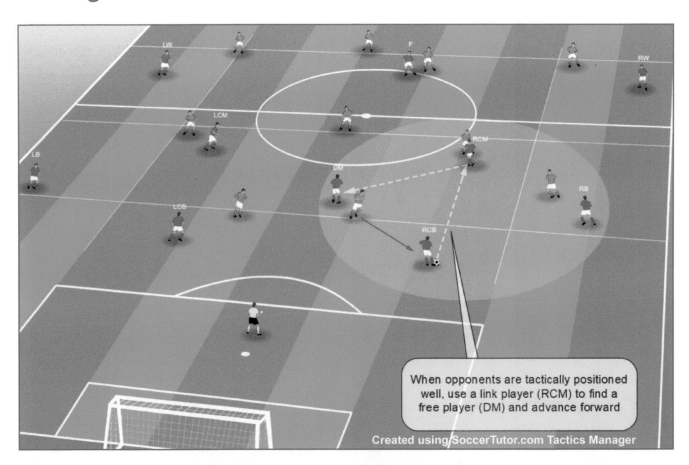

When opponents are tactically positioned well, use a link player (RCM) to find a free player (DM) and advance forward

Created using SoccerTutor.com Tactics Manager

This can be done if the player in possession of the ball (RCB) passes to the central midfielder (RCM) at the top of the rhombus, who, in turn, redirects the ball to the defensive midfielder (DM).

Naturally, the centre back in possession of the ball (RCB) can also use a back pass to the goalkeeper, in case the passing lane toward the top of the rhombus (RCM in this case) is blocked.

Indirect ways for connecting a pass with a key teammate is important to avoid pressure when building up play from the back.

The pass from the centre back (RCB) to the right central midfielder (RCM) shown in the diagram above demonstrates the pivotal role of the latter as a link player.

Using a "Link Player" to Get Around the Pressing of Our Centre Back Against 1 Forward

If we face an opponent with 5 midfielders and one forward, in order to play a link pass to a teammate positioned behind the opposition's midfield line, we must first "force" an opposing midfielder to leave their midfield line, then pass the ball to our player freed by the move just described.

As seen before, the opponents will try to put pressure on the player in possession of the ball, trying to block the passing lane to his free teammate at the same time.

In the 2 diagrams (Option 1 and Option 2), we show how to resolve this situation when an opposing midfielder moves forward to put pressure on our centre back, who is advancing with the ball.

OPTION 1: Defensive Midfielder is the "Link Player"

The DM is the link player used to advance forward to the unmarked LCM

In this first example, our defensive midfielder (DM) is the "link player" used to move the ball to our left central midfielder (LCM). He is able to receive unmarked, turn and progress the attack.

OPTION 2: Forward is the "Link Player"

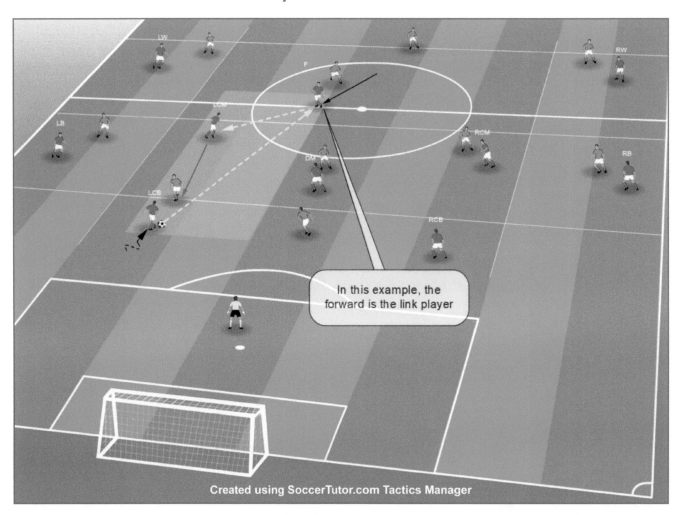

In this example, the forward is the link player

Created using SoccerTutor.com Tactics Manager

In this second example, the forward is the "link player" used to move the ball to our left central midfielder (LCM), who is left unmarked. He can again receive in space and progress the attack.

2. BUILD UP PLAY AGAINST TEAMS THAT PRESS WITH THEIR FORWARDS & MIDFIELD (NO SPACE IN BEHIND)

2. BUILD UP PLAY AGAINST TEAMS THAT PRESS WITH THEIR FORWARDS & MIDFIELD (NO SPACE IN BEHIND)

The goalkeeper starts with a short pass and the opposition are using an aggressive approach, with their forwards and midfielders pressing high up the pitch. The opposing defenders support the approach, but do not push up to try and win the ball themselves. Therefore, they are still fairly deep and there isn't much space left in behind for our attackers to exploit.

It is possible to penetrate the opposition's defence, starting with a forward pass toward one of our attackers (wingers or forward), who can drop back to receive a pass between the opposition's midfield and defensive lines (see diagram below).

Passing Through the Midfield Line Against the 4-5-1

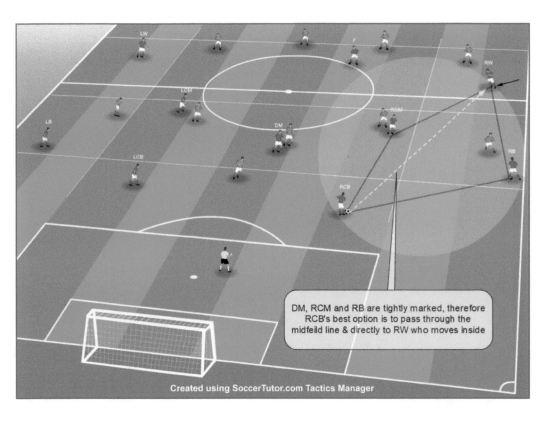

DM, RCM and RB are tightly marked, therefore RCB's best option is to pass through the midfeild line & directly to RW who moves inside

Created using SoccerTutor.com Tactics Manager

Against a team using 1 forward (in this instance the 4-5-1 formation), it is the centre back who comes out with the ball free of marking.

If the defensive midfielder (DM), full back (RB) and the central midfielder on that side (RCM) are all tightly marked by their direct opponents, the best solution is to play a forward pass to the winger on that side (RW), who moves inside and drops off to receive in between the lines.

This pass from the centre back (RCB) to the winger (RW) takes advantage of the opposition's tactical organisation, as they are unable to mark players tightly in between their midfield and defensive lines. This is because their defensive line is relatively deep, to prevent long passes being played into the space in their half.

The winger can receive and turn. The team now have an advantageous situation to attack the opposition.

Passing Through the Midfield Line Against the 4-3-1-2

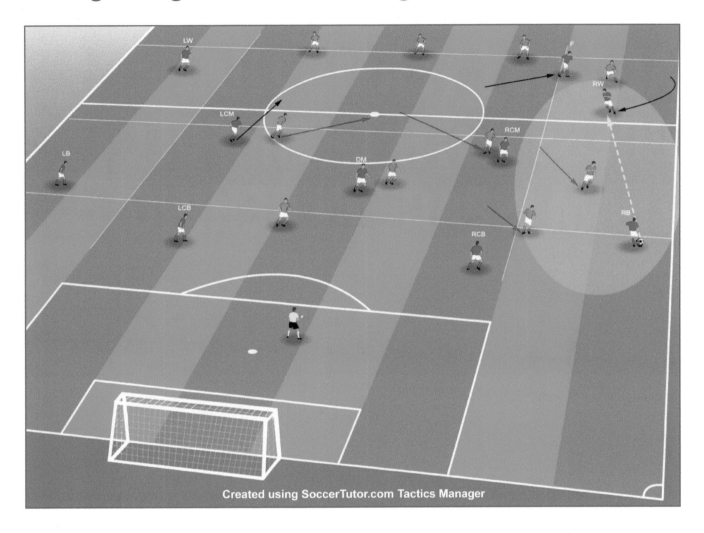

Against a team using a 4-3-1-2 formation, the pass from our back line could again be directed to the winger dropping back, similar to the situation shown in the previous diagram against the 4-5-1.

In this situation, the full back (RB) has possession of the ball and not the centre back. Due to this, the opposition players have shifted across to that side of the pitch.

The right back (RB) passes to the right winger (RW), who drops off to receive in space and turn.

3. DIRECT BUILD UP PLAY AGAINST TEAMS THAT PRESS WITH THEIR FULL TEAM (SPACE IN BEHIND)

3. DIRECT BUILD UP PLAY AGAINST TEAMS THAT PRESS WITH THEIR FULL TEAM (SPACE IN BEHIND)

If the opposition press forward with their whole team (e.g. When they are losing), our best option is to use a direct attack. This is the most logical and appropriate action.

If, following short distribution at the back, we see our opponents starting an all-out press with their defensive players marking our forwards in a very aggressive way, and even taking chances, trying to beat our forwards to the ball by anticipating passes towards them, we play the ball directly to our attackers (wingers and forward).

Direct build-up is used when the whole opposing team is pushed forward, with the defensive line near the halfway line. The attackers make short-long moves (check away from marker before making deep run) to receive the ball in behind the opposition's defensive line.

However, we must keep in mind that this attacking approach will "extend" our team (a less compact team becomes more vulnerable) and forces a faster pace that requires more energy to be sustained over a long period of time.

The diagrams to follow display our solutions for this tactical situation. As mentioned above, these solutions must be considered when the opposition don't give us enough space to build up play.

In the first situation shown in the diagram below, the long pass is played from the back line via the full back (RB) and the aim is to directly exploit the space in the opposition's half.

Direct Pass for the Winger in Behind the Defensive Line

Against high pressing team, a long pass behind the defensive line is a good option

Created using SoccerTutor.com Tactics Manager

Using the Forward as a "Link Player" to Pass to the Winger

The same principle, this time using the forward as the "link player"

Created using SoccerTutor.com Tactics Manager

As in the previous example, the right winger (RW) makes the same run in behind, but this is a slight variation with the forward acting as a "link player."

For this variation, the RW would have to adjust the timing of their run.

Using the Winger as a "Link Player" to Pass to the Forward

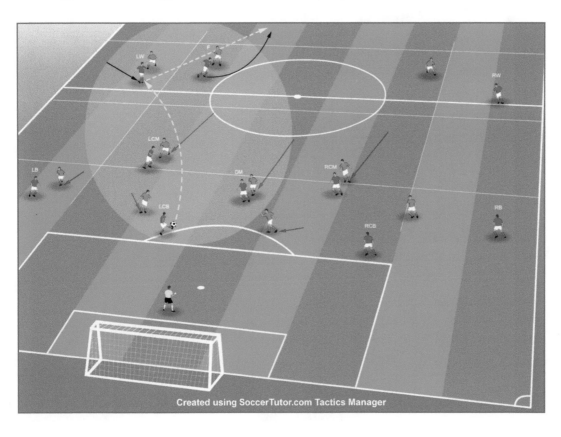

Created using SoccerTutor.com Tactics Manager

In this variation, the winger (LW) moves inside to receive a long pass and then pass to the forward (F) in behind the defensive line.

CHAPTER 3

BUILD UP PLAY AGAINST DIFFERENT FORMATIONS

BUILD UP PLAY AGAINST DIFFERENT FORMATIONS

GOALKEEPER'S DISTRIBUTION FROM GOAL KICKS AND BUILD UP PLAY FROM THE BACK

The strategy for the goalkeeper's distribution follows those that we fully explained in Chapter 1.

If the goalkeeper has used a short pass distribution, the team will then have to be able to advance up the pitch by utilising the pattern of play most appropriate to the tactical situation on the pitch.

The team must know and must be able to apply solutions for the following different situations:

- **Attacking against opponents that withdraw into their half and DEFEND DEEP**

- **Attacking against opponents with a 4 MAN DEFENCE (4-4-2, 4-4-1-1 or 4-2-3-1, 4-3-1-2 & 4-3-3)**

- **Attacking against opponents with a 3 MAN DEFENCE (3-4-3 & 3-5-2)**

BUILD UP PLAY AGAINST THE 4-4-2

BUILD UP PLAY AGAINST THE 4-4-2

If the opposition are using the 4-4-2 system, it's of fundamental importance to exploit the numerical advantage in the centre of the pitch. We should look to play to the defensive midfielder (DM) free in space.

Centre Back in Possession: Free Pass to the Defensive Midfielder in Space

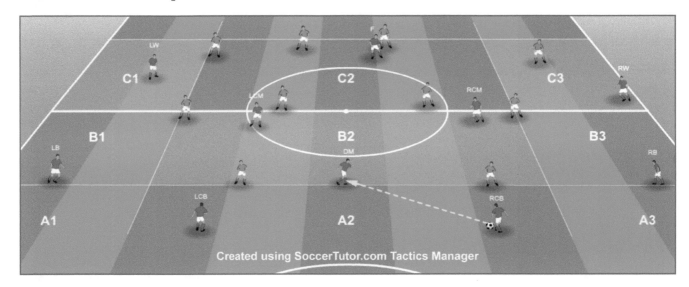

If the opponents line up with 2 forwards, we must move the ball past the first opposing line by passing to the defensive midfielder (DM). In this example, the ball is in possession of the right centre back (RCB). The focus is on moving the ball from Zone A2 to B2. The centre back (RCB) passes into Zone B2 and the defensive midfielder (DM) is able to receive in space and look up/forward to advance the play.

What are the Options for the Defensive Midfielder?

1. **Pass in Front of the Midfield Line:**

   - Pass to the closest central midfielder.

   - Pass out wide to the full back when the opposition withdraw to defend in their own half (**see example on page 43**).

2. **Playing in Between the Midfield and Defensive Lines:**

   - In collaboration with the CM on the other side or with the front support, pass to the CM who has moved beyond the opposition's midfield line (**see example on page 44**).

   - Pass to the winger's feet on the flank. This option can be taken if the opposing wide

   player is not positioned well and unable to intercept the potential pass.

3. **Long Pass in Behind the Defensive Line:**

   - This is a long pass in behind for the forward who makes a run and attacks the space. This option is taken when a gap is created in the opposition defence or if their defence is slow or unbalanced (**see example on page 45**).

4. **Restart the Attack by Passing Back:**

   - Pass the ball back to a centre back.

   - Pass the ball back to the goalkeeper.

I. PASS IN FRONT OF THE MIDFIELD LINE:
Tactical Solution Against Teams That Withdraw into their Own Half and Defend Deep

Created using SoccerTutor.com Tactics Manager

After the pass shown on the previous page, the defensive midfielder (DM) is in possession of the ball and looking to advance his team's attack.

If the defending team decide to withdraw (drop back) into their own half in order to tighten their midfield and defensive lines, the defensive midfielder (DM) should pass the ball to a teammate on one of the flanks. This will most likely be to the full back (LB in diagram) or winger.

The choice of who to pass to on the flank depends whether there is an available passing line towards the winger.

Alternatively, the DM can play a short pass to the closest central midfielder - this would be the left central midfielder (LCM) in the diagram example.

2. PLAYING IN BETWEEN THE MIDFIELD AND DEFENSIVE LINES: Exploiting Pressing to Play to Central Midfielder Who Makes a Forward Run in Between the Lines

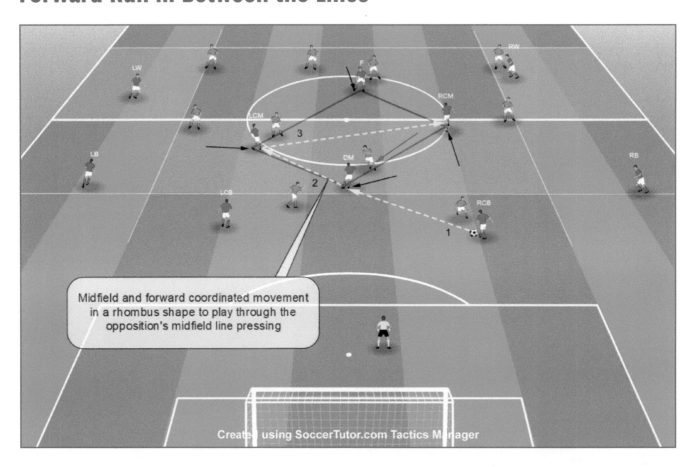

Midfield and forward coordinated movement in a rhombus shape to play through the opposition's midfield line pressing

The defensive midfielder (DM) is in possession of the ball, looking to advance and take advantage of the opposition's pressing. The team use coordinated movement in the centre of the pitch to create space and then receive in between the midfield and defensive lines.

It is important to "build" a rhombus shape with the central midfielders moving in opposite directions (one moves forward, one drops back) and the forward functioning as frontal support.

In this example, the right central midfielder (RCM) is the one that moves forward. This is because the opposing player who was previously marking him moves away to press the ball carrier (our DM).

The left central midfielder (LCM) makes the opposite movement and drops back slightly, moving closer to the defensive midfielder (DM) in possession of the ball. The LCM receives the short pass from the DM and quickly passes to the RCM, who has moved beyond the opposition's midfield line.

The formation of the rhombus shape helps the indirect movement of the ball from the defensive midfielder (DM) to the right central midfielder (RCM) via the left central midfielder (LCM), who acts as the "link player."

If the LCM is under too much pressure from his direct opponent to receive in space, the DM can connect directly with the frontal support (forward), who can then act as the "link player" to play the ball back to the RCM, who is unmarked.

Another alternative is to pass directly to one of the wingers. However, this is only possible if the opposing wide player is not positioned well and is unable to intercept the potential pass.

3. LONG PASS IN BEHIND THE DEFENSIVE LINE:
Exploiting the Space When a Gap is Created in the Opposition's Defence

In this variation, the centre back presses our RCM, which creates a gap for our forward (F) to exploit

Created using SoccerTutor.com Tactics Manager

In this variation, the opposing centre back moves forward to mark our right central midfielder (RCM), so we no longer have the objective to pass to him.

Although one option is now blocked, a gap in the opposition's defence has been created. Our defensive midfielder (DM) therefore plays a long pass into this gap and in behind for our forward to run onto.

If the pass and run in behind are well timed, the forward could be left with a 1 v 1 against the goalkeeper and a goal scoring opportunity.

BUILD UP PLAY AGAINST THE 4-4-1-1 OR 4-2-3-1

BUILD UP PLAY AGAINST THE 4-4-1-1 or 4-2-3-1

When the oppositions have 1 centre forward and a No.10 (attacking midfielder), the No.10 marks our defensive midfielder (DM). It is important to exploit this situation by having one of the centre backs (who have a 2 v 1 numerical advantage against the forward) dribble the ball forward past the first line of the opposition - this is shown in the diagram below with RCB moving from Zone A2 to B2.

Centre Back Dribbling the Ball Out of Defence

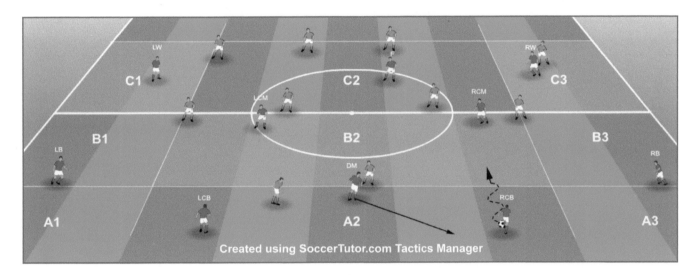

Created using SoccerTutor.com Tactics Manager

In this example, our left centre back (LCB) and defensive midfielder (DM) are tightly marked by the opposing forward and No.10. The right centre back (RCB) has the ball free in space, so dribbles forward. The defensive midfielder (DM) drops back to cover RCB's position. This movement enables us to move the ball from Zone A2 to B2. How we advance from this point depends on the positioning and reactions of our opponents.

What are the Options for the Centre Back?

Depending on the positioning and reactions of the opposition players, RCB has the following options:

1. Pass in Front of the Midfield Line:

- Pass to central midfielder on the opposite side.
- Pass out wide to the full back on the same side.

2. Playing in Between the Midfield and Defensive Lines:

- In collaboration with the winger and the central midfielder on the other side, pass to the CM who has moved beyond the opposition's midfield line (**see example on page 49**).

3. Long Pass in Behind the Defensive Line:

- This is a long pass in behind for the forward who makes a run and attacks the space. This option is taken when a gap is created in the opposition defence or if their defence is slow, unbalanced or unprepared (**see example on page 50**).

4. Restart the Attack by Passing Back:

- Pass the ball back to a centre back.
- Pass the ball back to the goalkeeper.

I. PASS IN FRONT OF THE MIDFIELD LINE:
Tactical Solution Against Teams That Withdraw into their Own Half and Defend Deep

Created using SoccerTutor.com Tactics Manager

The right centre back (RCB) dribbles out of defence, as shown on the previous page.

If the defending team decide to withdraw (drop back) into their own half in order to tighten their midfield and defensive lines, the RCB should pass the ball to a teammate on one of the flanks, most likely to the full back (RB in diagram) or winger.

The choice of who to pass to on the flank depends whether there is an available passing line towards the winger.

Alternatively, the RCB can play a short pass to the closest central midfielder - this would be the right central midfielder (RCM) in the diagram example.

2. PLAYING IN BETWEEN THE MIDFIELD AND DEFENSIVE LINES:
Exploiting Pressing to Play to Central Midfielder Who Makes a Forward Run in Between the Lines

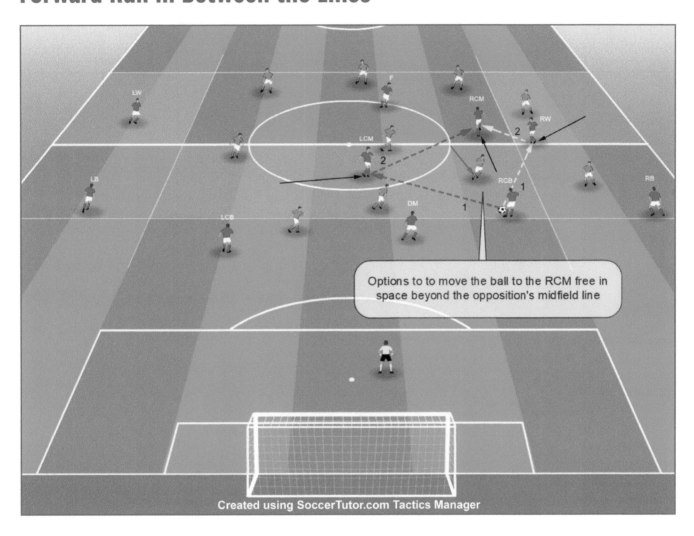

Options to to move the ball to the RCM free in space beyond the opposition's midfield line

As the centre back (RCB) dribbles forward, the right central midfielder (RCM) moves forward beyond the opposition's midfield line and acts as the front support in the rhombus shape.

The left central midfielder (LCM) and the right winger (RW) move inwards from their positions respectively, to act as the side supports in the rhombus shape.

As soon as the opposing central midfielder moves to press the ball carrier (our DM), the objective is to move the ball to the RCM free in space beyond the opposition's midfield line.

This can be done by passing to either side support player (LCM or RW) and they act as "link players" to move the ball to the RCM, who receives beyond the opposition's midfield line.

If these options are unavailable, RCB can pass to the full back on the same side (RB) who stays wide to provide an additional option to the centre back.

3. LONG PASS IN BEHIND THE DEFENSIVE LINE:
Exploiting the Space When a Gap is Created in the Opposition's Defence

In this variation, the centre back presses our RCM, which creates a gap for our forward (F) to exploit

Created using SoccerTutor.com Tactics Manager

In this variation, the opposing centre back moves forward to mark our right central midfielder (RCM), so we no longer have the objective to pass to him.

Although one option is now blocked, a gap in the opposition's defence has been created. Our centre back (RCB) therefore plays a long pass into this gap and in behind for our forward to run onto.

If the pass and run in behind are well timed, the forward could be left with a 1 v 1 against the goalkeeper and a goal scoring opportunity.

BUILD UP PLAY AGAINST THE 4-3-1-2

BUILD UP PLAY AGAINST THE 4-3-1-2

When playing against the 4-3-1-2, the opposition have 2 forwards, a No.10 and 3 midfielders. They have a diamond midfield with no wide players and their No.10 marks our defensive midfielder (DM). In order to organise an effective attacking move, it is very important to first direct the ball toward the full back.

Full Back Receives in Space Out Wide

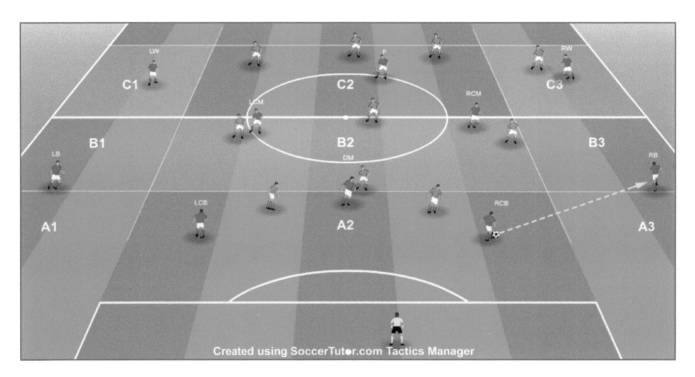

Created using SoccerTutor.com Tactics Manager

What are the Options for the Full Back?

Depending on the positioning and reactions of the opposition players, the full back in possession (RB in diagram) has the following options:

1. Pass in Front of the Midfield Line:

* 1-2 combination with the defensive midfielder to move the ball to the central midfielder free in the centre (**see example on page 53**).

2. Long Pass in Behind the Defensive Line:

* This is a long pass in behind for the forward who makes a run and attacks the space. This happens specifically when the opposing centre back leaves his position to mark our winger, who cuts inside (**see example on page 54**).

3. Switch Play to the Weak Side:

* The opposing full back and centre back stay in position. Our first aim is to play a direct pass to the winger ("imbucata" - entry ball), who could receive between the lines.

* However, this option may be blocked, so we can switch play to the full back who is free in space (**see example on page 55**).

4. Restart the Attack by Passing Back:

* Pass the ball back to a centre back.
* Pass the ball back to the goalkeeper.

I. PASS IN FRONT OF THE MIDFIELD LINE:
1-2 Combination with the Defensive Midfielder to Move the Ball to the Central Midfielder Free in the Middle

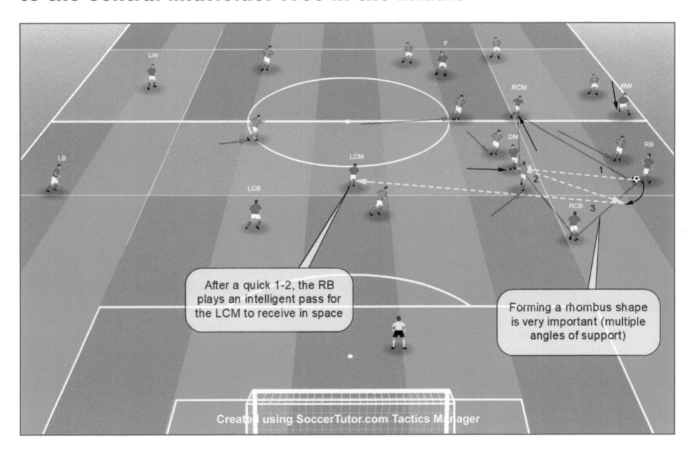

After a quick 1-2, the RB plays an intelligent pass for the LCM to receive in space

Forming a rhombus shape is very important (multiple angles of support)

After the pass shown on the previous page, the right back (RB) is in possession of the ball, looking to advance his team's attack.

When the ball is in the full back's possession (RB in diagram), it is very important to form a rhombus shape with the following movements:

- The central midfielder on that side (RCM) moves forward and beyond the opposition's midfield line into the front support position of the rhombus.

- The defensive midfielder moves closer to the full back (RB) and provides side support.

- The centre back (RCB) provides back support to complete the rhombus shape.

In addition, shifting our midfielders into 2 lines (with different depths) forces the opponents to make some quick decisions.

For example, our winger (RW) drops back and the opposing left back has to decide whether to follow him or stay back to retain stability in the back line. If he stays back, our winger (RW) could easily receive a pass from our right back (RB) - this would create a new rhombus shape without the need for the RCB, as the RB would now be at the base of it.

As explained on the previous page, when playing against the 4-3-1-2, our defensive midfielder (DM) is being marked by their No.10. In this tactical example, the right back decides to play a 1-2 combination with the defensive midfielder (DM).

After playing the return pass, the DM moves forward a little to create space for the next pass from the right back (RB) to the left central midfielder (LCM). The LCM is able to receive in space in the centre unmarked.

2. LONG PASS IN BEHIND THE DEFENSIVE LINE:
Exploiting Space when the Opposing Defenders Step Up to Press

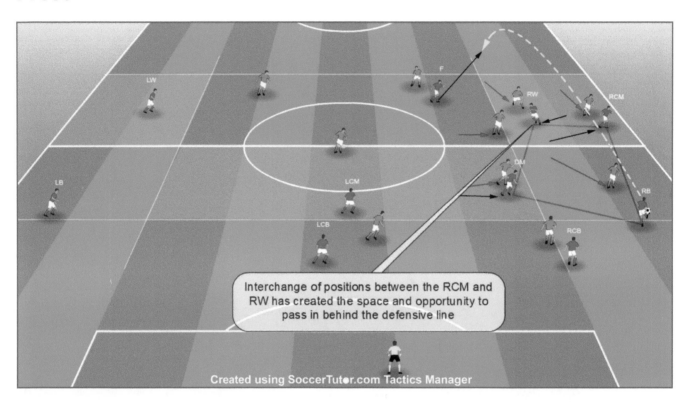

Interchange of positions between the RCM and RW has created the space and opportunity to pass in behind the defensive line

Created using SoccerTutor.com Tactics Manager

In this tactical example, the opponents have different reactions that change our decision making. Playing a direct pass in behind the defensive line is Plan B.

The rhombus shape we form is different to the one in the previous example. This time, the right central midfielder (RCM) moves wide and the right winger (RW) moves inside. The winger therefore takes the position of front support in the rhombus. The defensive midfielder (DM) who moves across and the RCM are the side supports in the rhombus. The forward stands right on the opposition's defensive line, so that the distances between their midfield and defensive lines are extended as much as possible. He stands ready to exploit a direct pass in behind.

The opponents have different decisions to make in relation to adjustments and movements. Our player in possession (RB) will have to be ready to choose the most appropriate attacking solution.

The first decision the opponents have to make relates to the marking of our right central midfielder (RCM) who has moved toward the sideline.

In particular, it's the opposing left back who has to decide between 2 options:

1. Follow the RW's movement inside:

Clearly, if the opposing left back decided to follow our winger (RW) cutting inside, the player in possession of the ball (RB) would pass directly (or indirectly via a link player) to the RCM.

2. Stay in position and contest RCM who moves out wide:

If the opposing left back remains in his zone, the winger who cut inside will most likely be marked by the opposing left centre back. This centre back would have to move forward.

In this situation, the ball carrier (RB) and the forward can act quickly to exploit the imbalance created in the opposition's defensive line.

As shown in the diagram, the right back (RB) plays a long pass in behind for the forward to run onto and receive in behind. If the run and pass are well timed, this could lead to a 1 v 1 against the goalkeeper and a goal scoring opportunity.

3. PASSING OPTIONS BLOCKED: Switch Play to the Weak Side

In this situation, switching play to the weak side is the best option

CB stays, therefore the long pass in behind is not a good option

Created using SoccerTutor.com Tactics Manager

In this variation of the previous tactical example, the opposing left centre back does not move forward and out of position. Therefore, the option to play a direct pass in behind the defensive line to the forward, as shown on the previous page, is no longer a good idea.

In this situation, our first choice would be to play a direct pass to the RW ("imbucata" - entry ball), who could receive between the lines. However, in this specific example shown in the diagram, the opposition's central midfielder is able to quickly move across to mark our winger (RW). In addition, the opposing left back is marking our RCM.

As our right back (RB) is unable to pass to the winger (RW), the objective changes to switching play for a wide attack on the "weak" side, after moving the ball in front of the opposing midfielders and counting on the ability of our defender (LB) on that side to receive and start dribbling the ball forward.

Specifically, in this tactical example shown in the diagram, the right back (RB) plays a 1-2 with the defensive midfielder (as he is marked by the opposition's No.10) and moves slightly back to receive the return pass.

After playing the return pass, the DM moves forward a little to create space for the next pass from the right back (RB) to the left central midfielder (LCM).

The LCM is able to receive in space in the centre unmarked and then complete the switch of play with a pass to the left back (LB), who can dribble forward into the space on the weak side.

BUILD UP PLAY AGAINST THE 4-3-3

BUILD UP PLAY AGAINST THE 4-3-3

When we face an opponent with the same formation (4-3-3), it's important to build up play from the back, taking advantage of the numerical superiority in the middle (our 2 centre backs vs. 1 forward). One of our centre backs can advance with the ball easily, moving from Zone A2 to B2.

Centre Back Dribbling the Ball Out of Defence

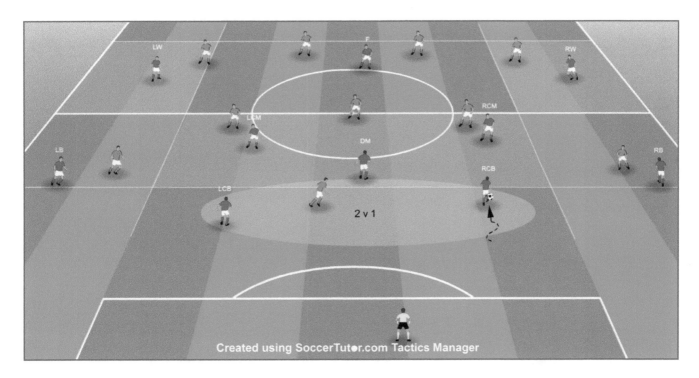

What are the Options for the Centre Back?

Depending on the positioning and reactions of the opposition players, the centre back (RCB) has the following options:

1. **Pass in Front of the Midfield Line:**

   - Short pass to the defensive midfielder or a central midfielder when an opposing central midfielder moves forward to press the ball (**see example on page 58**).

2. **Switch Play to Attack on Opposite Side:**

   - Pass to the DM when the opposition withdraw to defend in their own half and develop an attack on the opposite side with rotation movements (**see example on page 59**).

3. **Playing in Between the Midfield and Defensive Lines:**

   - When there is aggressive pressing of the ball carrier and short passing options are blocked, play direct to the forward, who acts as a "link player" to move the ball to the advancing central midfielder (**see example on page 60**).

4. **Restart the Attack by Passing Back:**

   - Pass to the full back on the same side when the opposing winger moves inside to block the forward passing lane.

   - Pass the ball to the goalkeeper or a centre back who frees himself from the opposing forward.

I. PASS IN FRONT OF THE MIDFIELD LINE:
Exploiting the Pressing of the Opposing Central Midfielder to Play Short Pass to a Teammate in Space

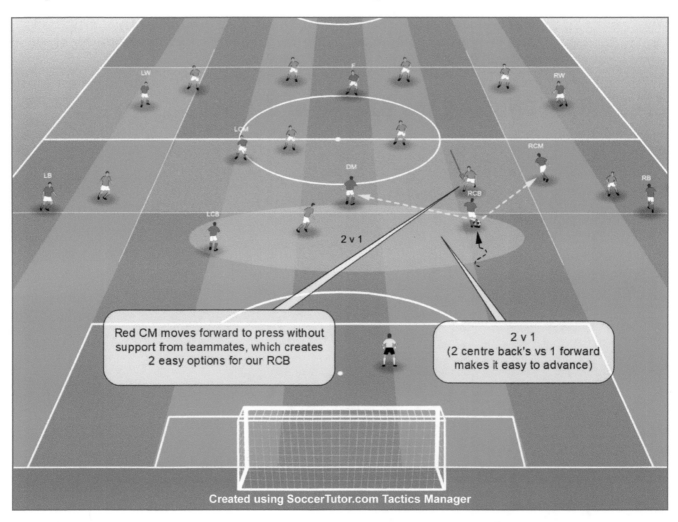

Red CM moves forward to press without support from teammates, which creates 2 easy options for our RCB

2 v 1
(2 centre back's vs 1 forward makes it easy to advance)

Created using SoccerTutor.com Tactics Manager

As explained on the previous page, our centre backs have a 2 v 1 advantage against the opposing forward, so 1 centre back (RCB in diagram example) can dribble the ball forward easily.

As the RCB moves forward with the ball, an opposing central midfielder moves forward to press him. However, he does not receive pressing support from his teammates.

The right centre back (RCB) therefore has 2 easy passing options:

1. Pass to the left of the opposing midfielder to the defensive midfielder (DM) in space in the centre.

2. Pass to the right of the opposing midfielder to the right central midfielder (RCM), who is also in space.

The team can then advance their attack from there, with 4 opposition players now behind the line of the ball.

A third option may be to combine with the defensive midfielder to play the ball to the other central midfielder (LCM).

2. SWITCH PLAY TO ATTACK ON OPPOSITE SIDE:
Tactical Solution Against Teams That Withdraw into their Own Half and Defend Deep

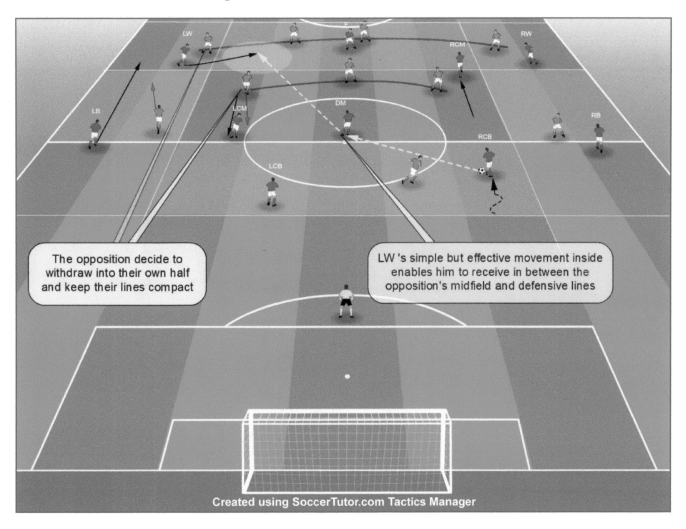

The opposition decide to withdraw into their own half and keep their lines compact

LW 's simple but effective movement inside enables him to receive in between the opposition's midfield and defensive lines

Created using SoccerTutor.com Tactics Manager

If the opposition decide to withdraw into their own half and keep their lines compact, our attacking move will have to be developed on the flanks.

In this tactical example, the right centre back (RCB) can easily pass to the defensive midfielder (DM) in space in the centre. From here, the team can develop their attack on the opposite side.

The left central midfielder (LCM), the left back (LB) and the left winger (LW) all make rotational movements, as shown in the diagram. These are made to move away from their markers, create space and try to receive a pass from the defensive midfielder (DM).

In the diagram example, the left winger (LW) is able to receive in between the opposition's midfield and defensive lines after moving inside.

3. PLAYING IN BETWEEN THE MIDFIELD AND DEFENSIVE LINES:
Exploiting Aggressive Pressing to Play to Central Midfielder via the Forward

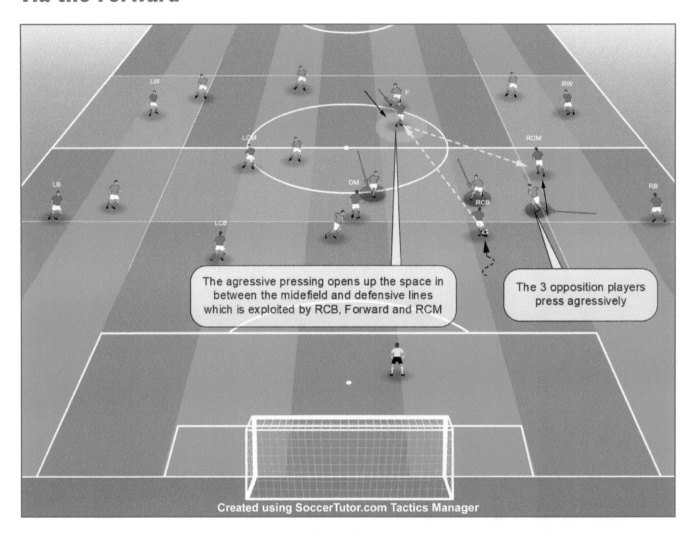

The agressive pressing opens up the space in between the midfield and defensive lines which is exploited by RCB, Forward and RCM

The 3 opposition players press agressively

Created using SoccerTutor.com Tactics Manager

If our opponent uses aggressive pressing, we look to pass in between the midfield and defensive lines.

In this tactical example, the opposing LCM has moved forward to press the ball carrier (our centre back - RCB) and the opposing defensive midfielder has moved forward to mark our defensive midfielder (DM).

The opposing winger has also moved inside to block the passing line from our RCB to our RCM.

The best solution to this problem is to play the ball to the RCM beyond the opposition's midfield line via a "link player" (the forward).

The right central midfielder (RCM) moves forward but the passing line towards him is blocked. The right centre back (RCB) therefore passes to the forward who drops off. The forward is closely marked but is able to play the ball back to the oncoming RCM.

The RCM has successfully received between the lines and our team are in a good position for an attack.

BUILD UP PLAY AGAINST THE 3-4-3

BUILD UP PLAY AGAINST THE 3-4-3

Positioning Against the 3-4-3 Before the Opposition Make Defensive Adjustments

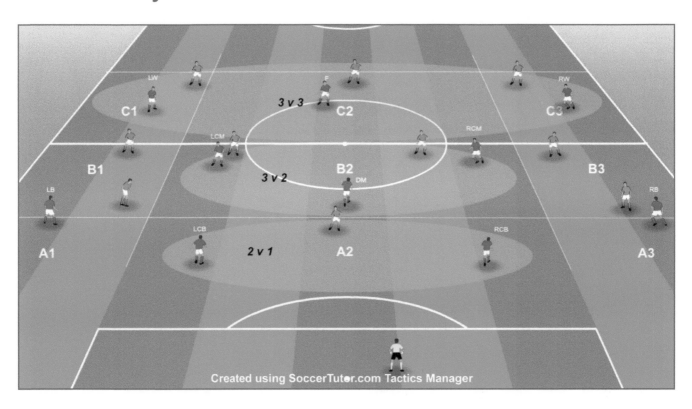

Most of the time when teams using the 4-3-3 formation line-up against the 3-4-3 formation, the opposition have to make adjustments. This is because of the following numerical disadvantages they would have in different zones of the pitch:

- **Zone A2:** Our centre backs have a 2 v 1 numerical advantage against the opposing forward. This means that our centre backs would have few difficulties building up play, as there should always be a spare player who can simply move forward with the ball.

- **Zone B2:** Our DM and 2 central midfielders have a 3 v 2 numerical advantage against the 2 central midfielders of the opposing team. This means that there should always be a spare player to receive a pass in space (unmarked), thus making it relatively easy to play through this zone and toward the wingers or forward.

- **Zones C1-C3:** Our 3 attackers (wingers and forward) have a numerical equality against the 3 defenders. This would mean that a long pass could easily lead to a 3 v 3 attack in the opposition's half, with the opportunity to exploit 1 v 1 situations.

The Opposition Make Tactical Adjustments from the 3-4-3 Formation to the 4-3-3

As explained on the previous page, if the opposition remained in their 3-4-3 formation during their defensive phase and didn't make any tactical adjustments, our players would have few difficulties building up play from the back (2 v 1 advantage in Zone A2, 3 v 2 advantage in Zone B2 and 3 v 3 advantage in Zone C which creates 1 v 1 situations).

The diagram above shows a classic tactical adjustment of the opposition in this situation. They change their defensive formation from a 3-4-3 to a 4-3-3 with the following 2 movements:

1. One of the wide midfielders from the midfield 4 (right in diagram) drops back to create a back 4 for his team. This means that there is now a 4 v 3 numerical disadvantage for our attackers. Therefore, we will not be able to exploit 1 v 1 situations after a long pass into Zone C.

2. The other wide midfielder (left) moves inside to create a central midfield 3. This means that it is now a 3 v 3 numerical equality in Zone B2 and it will be much more difficult to play beyond the opposition's midfield line.

The preferred patterns of play to build up from the back against an opponent using a 4-3-3 formation have already been displayed in the previous section - please refer to these for attacking solutions for this tactical situation.

The Opposition Make Tactical Adjustments from the 3-4-3 Formation to the 3-4-2-1

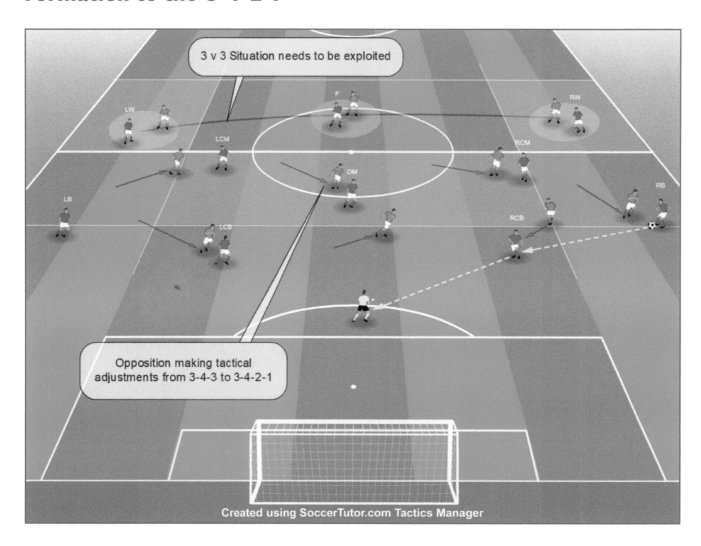

3 v 3 Situation needs to be exploited

Opposition making tactical adjustments from 3-4-3 to 3-4-2-1

Created using SoccerTutor.com Tactics Manager

The diagram above shows a second classic tactical adjustment of the opposition in this situation. They change their defensive formation from a 3-4-3 to a 3-4-2-1 with the following 2 movements:

1. The 2 outside forwards/wingers (left and right) move inwards toward the centre of the pitch.

2. The 2 wide midfielders (left and right) push up ready to apply pressure to our full backs.

When playing against teams defending in a 3-4-2-1 formation, they are usually willing to take many risks by implementing very aggressive pressing.

Naturally, it would be useless and counterproductive to try to build up play from the back when we have a numerical equality at the back (4 v 4). The opposition play man to man against our midfielders

and defenders, to prevent them from successfully building play from the back.

In this tactical example shown, our right back (RB) has the ball and we need to look to exploit a 3 v 3 situation in attack:

- Firstly, it is of fundamental importance to utilise our goalkeeper for support, as this is the only way to guarantee a numerical advantage at the back (5 v 4) - **see diagram above**.

- From this point, the goalkeeper can look to connect with the forwards using long passes or "imbucata" (entry balls) whenever it is possible. If one of our 3 attackers can receive, it will most likely be a 1 v 1 situation against their direct opponent and a 3 v 3 situation overall in attack.

BUILD UP PLAY AGAINST THE 3-5-2

BUILD UP PLAY AGAINST THE 3-5-2

Opposing Wing Backs Push Up to Mark Our Full Backs: Pass Back to Keeper for Long Pass to Forwards

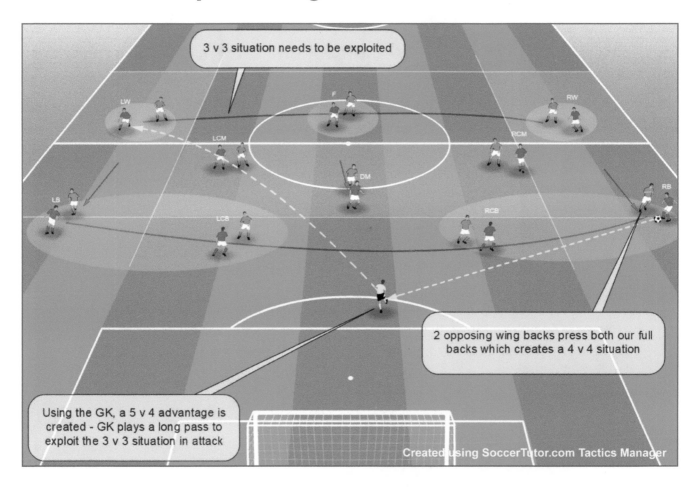

Against the 3-5-2 formation, it is again very important to find out whether the opposition are willing to face our forwards without a numerical advantage or not. Our decision making for building up play will change according to their tactical positioning during their defensive phase.

In this tactical example against the 3-5-2 formation, the opposing wing backs have moved forward and high up the pitch to mark our full backs and apply pressure.

This means that there is a 4 v 4 situation and a numerical equality for our defenders in the build up phase. This is dangerous and we need to create a numerical advantage at the back.

In this situation, our best strategy is shown in the diagram example. We must involve the goalkeeper in building up play from the back. This then creates a 5 v 4 numerical advantage and the player in possession can pass back to the goalkeeper.

In this specific example, the right back (RB) is put under pressure by the opposing wing back and passes back to the goalkeeper at the edge of the penalty area.

The goalkeeper then looks to play a long pass to exploit the 3 v 3 situation our attackers have against the opposing defenders. There is a good chance to then exploit 1 v 1 situations in attack.

Opposing Right Wing Back Moves Back to Create Back 4: Move the Ball to Our Left Back Free in Space

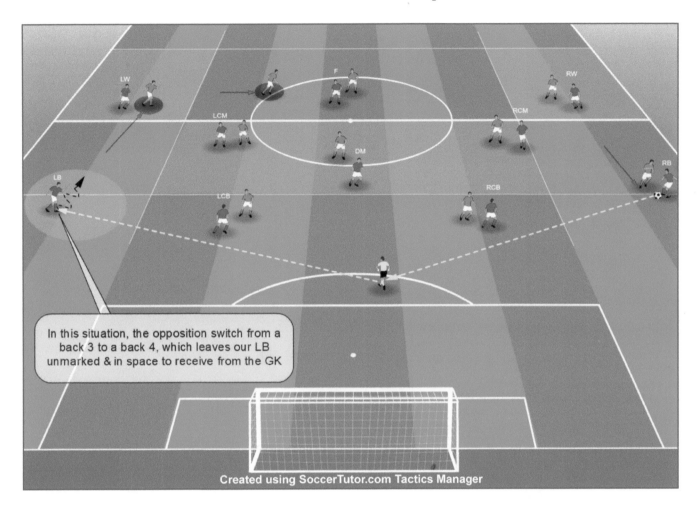

In this situation, the opposition switch from a back 3 to a back 4, which leaves our LB unmarked & in space to receive from the GK

Created using SoccerTutor.com Tactics Manager

As shown on the previous page, against the 3-5-2, we could potentially exploit a 3 v 3 numerical equality in attack via a long pass from the goalkeeper.

However, if the opponents take some precautions to ensure they have a numerical advantage at the back, we must work out what exact movements they are using so that we can determine the best solution.

In this tactical example, the red left wing back has pushed up to press our player in possession (RB) and the red right wing back has moved back to join the defensive line and create a 4 v 3 advantage for his team in Zone C. The opposition have now switched from a back 3 to a back 4.

In this situation, our objective is to move the ball to our left back (LB) who is unmarked and free to receive in space, possibly with the help of our goalkeeper if the central areas are too crowded.

In this specific example, the player in possession (RB) is under pressure and plays the ball back to the goalkeeper. The goalkeeper then passes the ball out wide to our left back (LB).

The left back is then able to dribble forward into the space ahead of him.

From this point, he has different options depending on the reactions of the opposing players. 2 of these options (tactical examples) are displayed on the next 2 pages:

1. **Playing in Between the Midfield and Defensive Lines: Exploit Pressing Depending On the Opposition's Reactions** (page 68)

2. **Long Pass in Behind the Defensive Line: Exploiting the Space When a Gap is Created in the Opposition's Defence** (page 69)

I. PLAYING IN BETWEEN THE MIDFIELD AND DEFENSIVE LINES:
Exploiting Pressing Depending on the Opposing Players' Reactions

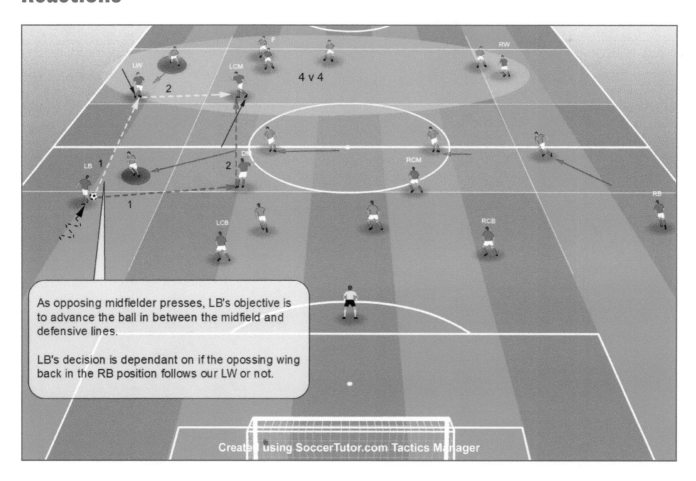

As opposing midfielder presses, LB's objective is to advance the ball in between the midfield and defensive lines.

LB's decision is dependant on if the opossing wing back in the RB position follows our LW or not.

Our team wants to make the correct decisions to advance the attack, in relation to the decision making of our opponents.

As our left back (LB) dribbles forward, it is highly likely that the opposing central midfielder will move wide and out of position to close him down.

In this tactical example, our left central midfielder (LCM) moves forward beyond the opposition's midfield line and acts as the front support in the rhombus shape.

The defensive midfielder (DM) is the right side support and the left winger (LW) drops back to act as the left side support in the rhombus shape.

As soon as the opposing central midfielder moves to press the ball carrier (our LB), the objective is to move the ball in between the opposition's midfield and defensive lines.

When the left winger (LW) drops back, he forces the opposing right wing back (who is now in the right back position - see previous page) to choose whether to follow him or to retain balance in defence for his team:

1. If the opposing player doesn't follow our winger (LW), the LB can make a simple forward pass for the LW to receive between the lines (**yellow passing lines in diagram**).

2. If the opposing player does follow our winger (LW), the LB passes inside to the defensive midfielder (DM), who then passes forward to the left central midfielder (LCM) in between the lines (**blue passing lines in diagram**).

With either scenario, our team would have an advantageous 4 v 4 situation to try and progress the attack.

2. LONG PASS IN BEHIND THE DEFENSIVE LINE:
Exploiting the Space When a Gap is Created in the Opposition's Defence

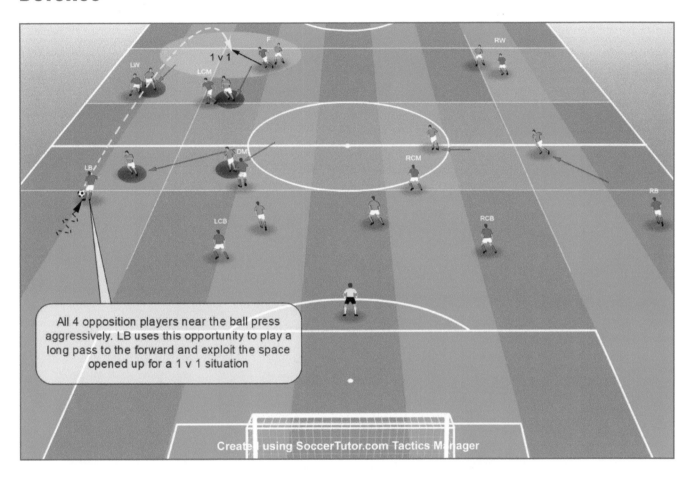

> All 4 opposition players near the ball press aggressively. LB uses this opportunity to play a long pass to the forward and exploit the space opened up for a 1 v 1 situation

Created using SoccerTutor.com Tactics Manager

The pattern of play shown in the example on the previous page demonstrates the importance of the centre forward's (F) position. He does not move towards the ball, but instead has a very important objective to keep the opposing defenders occupied. Otherwise, the opposing defenders could put pressure on our central midfielder (LCM), who has moved in between the lines.

However, there will be times when the opposition use an aggressive pressing tactic to mark all potential receivers and try to prevent our players from receiving between the lines. In these situations, we sometimes need to use a different tactic - a long pass in behind the defensive line.

In this tactical example, the opposing right centre back moves forward to mark our left central midfielder (LCM) and prevent him from receiving in between the lines. We no longer have the objective to pass to him via the defensive midfielder (DM).

In addition, the opposing defensive midfielder marks our defensive midfielder tightly and the opposing full back marks our left winger (LW) tightly.

Although both options to play in between the opposition's midfield and defensive lines (LCM and LW) are blocked, a gap in the opposition's defence has been created and our forward has a potential 1 v 1 situation against his direct opponent, with a lot of space to exploit in behind.

Our left back (LB) therefore plays a long pass into this gap and in behind for our forward to run onto.

If the pass and run are well timed, the forward could be left with a 1 v 1 against the goalkeeper and a goal scoring opportunity.

Opposing Defensive Midfielder Moves Back to Create Back 4: Move the Ball to Our Centre Back Who is Free in Space

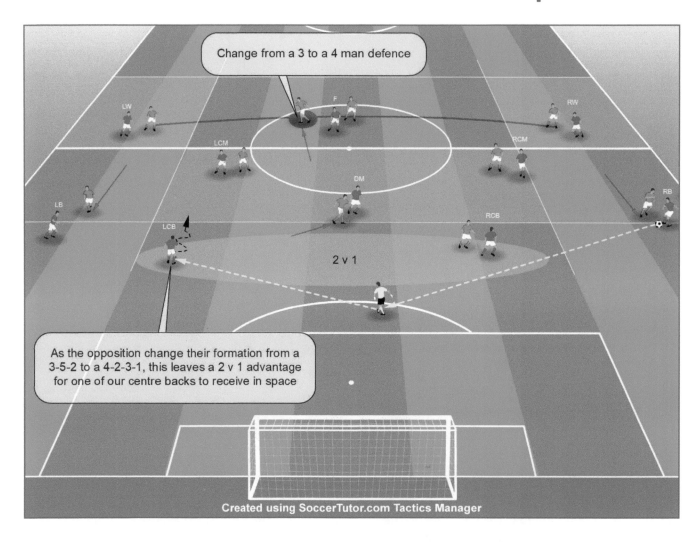

This shows a variation of the tactical situation on page 67.

The opposition again change their defensive shape to create a 4-man defence. However, this time it is their defensive midfielder who moves back to take up a centre back's position.

The opposition's 3-5-2 has now effectively changed to a 4-2-3-1 formation for the defensive phase.

We therefore exploit, the 2 v 1 advantage our centre backs have in Zone 2. One of the centre backs can receive and then dribble the ball forward.

To see the best patterns of play to use in this situation, see these 2 sections shown previously in this chapter:

- Attacking Against the 4-4-1-1 or 4-2-3-1

- Attacking Against the 4-3-3

PRACTICE EXAMPLES FOR BUILD UP PLAY

I. Goalkeeper's Distribution and Build Up Play from the Back in a 3 Zone II v 6 Practice

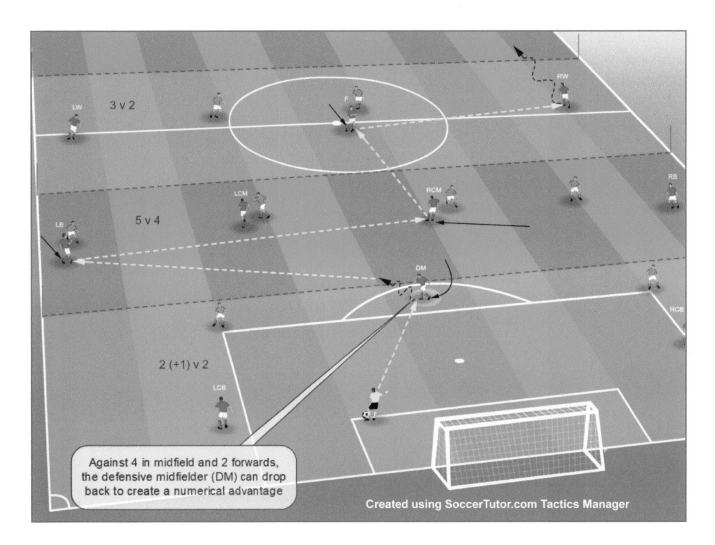

Against 4 in midfield and 2 forwards, the defensive midfielder (DM) can drop back to create a numerical advantage

Created using SoccerTutor.com Tactics Manager

Attacking Objective: Goalkeeper's distribution and build up play (moving through the lines).

Defending Objective: Active opposition during goal kick/throw + passive opposition during build up.

Practice Description

Using the area shown, we divide the area into 3 equal zones. The goalkeeper starts the practice by taking a goal kick or throwing the ball out to a teammate to start the build up.

The goalkeeper chooses the correct distribution based on the formation of the opposition. In the diagram example, the opposition (reds) are in a 4-2 formation, so the defensive midfielder (DM) drops back and we position our defence and midfield into a 3-4 formation. We therefore create a numerical advantage in the low zone and the goalkeeper can pass to the defensive midfielder, who is the spare man.

From this point, the blue team builds up play according to the instructions of the coach. The defending red team apply passive pressure. Once the blues have successfully played into the high zone, we restart the practice from the goalkeeper.

Progression: The defending team are fully active, try to stop the build up and then score a goal.

2. Goalkeeper's Distribution and Build Up Play from the Back in a 7 (+GK) v 6 Dynamic Game

Against a 3-3 formation, the LCM drops deep to create a numerical advantage (4 v 3) and receive from the GK

Objective: Building up play from the back into the opposition's half.

Practice Description

Using half a full pitch, we have the goalkeeper, the back 4 and 3 central midfielders from the 4-3-3 formation against 6 opposition players. In the diagram example, the red defending team are in a 3-3 formation. This can easily be changed to 4-2 or 3-1-2 etc.

The goalkeeper chooses the correct distribution based on the formation of the opposition. From this point, the blue team build up play and try to achieve one of these goals:

1. Score in one of the 3 mini goals on the halfway line.

2. Dribble the ball past the halfway line.

The red team aim to press collectively, stop the blue team from scoring and win the ball. If they win the ball, they then try to score in the big goal with a fast break attack.

3. Positional End to End Possession Game with Goalkeepers

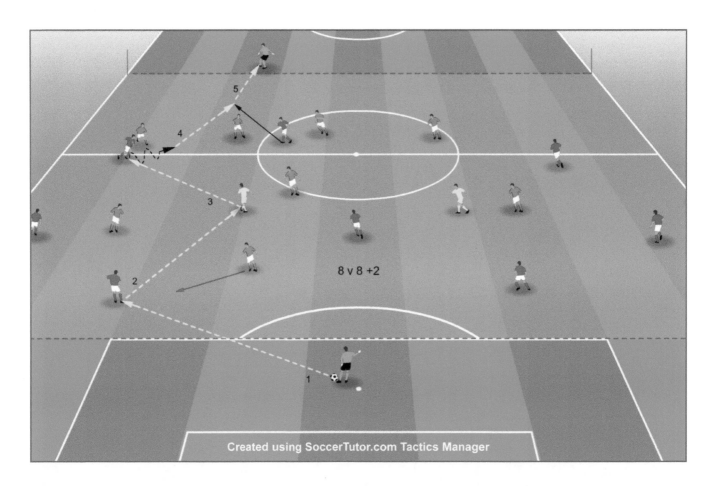

8 v 8 +2

Created using SoccerTutor.com Tactics Manager

Objective: Build up play from the back, possession play and positional play.

Practice Description

We mark out the area shown, with a goalkeeper outside at each end.

Each team has 8 outfield players and there are also 2 yellow neutral players, who take up the role of the central midfielders for the team in possession.

The practice starts from one goalkeeper and the team in possession (blues) are in a 4-3-3 formation with the 2 neutral players. The blues have an 11 v 8 numerical advantage (including GK).

These are the objectives for the team in possession (blues in diagram):

1. Complete 8 passes (1 point).

- If the defending team win the ball, the roles are simply reversed and the practice continues.

2. Move the ball from one goalkeeper to the other (1 point).

- After receiving the ball, the goalkeeper then gives the ball to the opponents (reds in diagram) and they continue with the same objectives, with the team roles reversed.

CHAPTER 4

THE CREATING PHASE

THE CREATING PHASE

After building up play with a short pass from our goalkeeper, we proceed with an effective passing game up to the midfield zone. The tactical context that we see at this point is the opposing team lined up according to their preferred formation, with almost all of their players inside their own half and behind the line of the ball.

The Opposition's Positioning During the Creating Phase

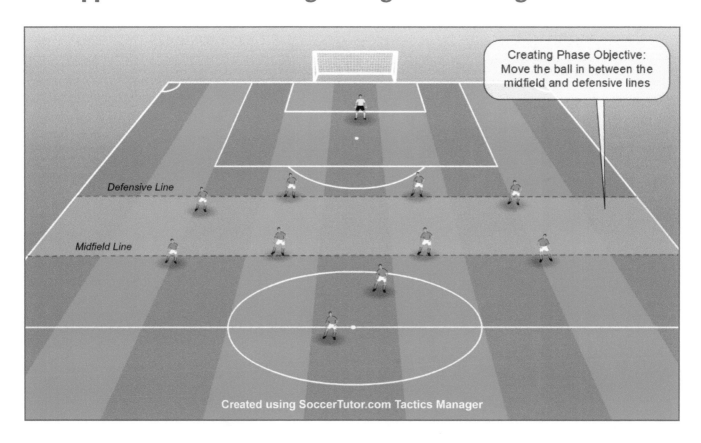

Creating Phase Objective: Move the ball in between the midfield and defensive lines

Defensive Line

Midfield Line

Created using SoccerTutor.com Tactics Manager

During our creating phase, the opposition set up in one of two ways:

1. **4-1-4-1 Formation**
   (as shown on page 78)

2. **4-4-1-1 Formation**
   (as shown in diagram above)

In this situation, the first objective is "Creating an Opening," ideally in behind the opposition's midfield line, where we can then dribble the ball forward or play a final pass.

Moving the ball in between the opposition's midfield and defensive lines is a fundamental condition needed for the team to then move into the next phase of "Accelerating the Attack."

I. CREATING AN OPENING (MOVING THE BALL TO THE WEAK SIDE)

I. CREATING AN OPENING (MOVING THE BALL TO THE WEAK SIDE)

To advance from one zone to the next (e.g. from the "Creating Zone to the "Finishing Zone" - see diagram below) and at the same time move the ball in between the opposition's midfield and defensive lines, a team can either: **Dribble the Ball Forward** or **Pass the Ball Forward** (directly or indirectly).

Pitch Zones and Sectors for "The Creating Phase"

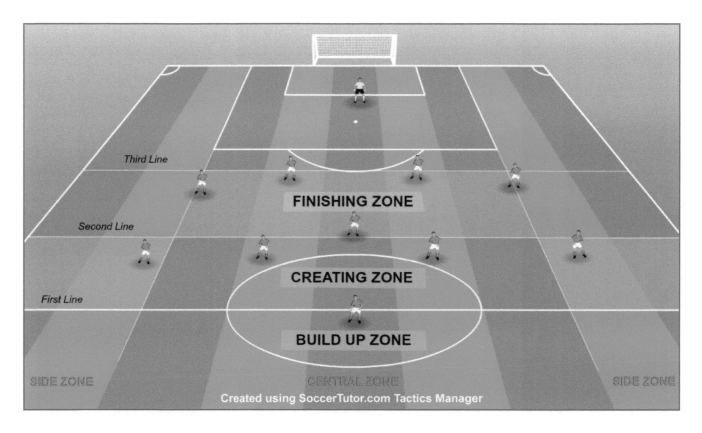

As mentioned previously, during our creating phase, the opposition set up in one of two ways:

1. **4-1-4-1 Formation**
   (as shown in diagram above)

2. **4-4-1-1 Formation**
   (as shown on page 76)

Naturally, the search for an opening in the opposition's defensive block and where to dribble or pass the ball must be a logical consequence of strategic ball movements, which have the objective of maintaining possession of the ball, while at the same time "force" movements of opposing players and opposing sectors.

"The Creating Phase" can be successful when we:

- Force the opposing players, who are initially organised into a compact formation, to move and eventually reconfirm their compact formation within a certain zone of the pitch.

- This creates space in other zones where we then aim to play the ball through rapid and accurate ball circulation (switching play to the weak side).

- Break the cohesion between opposing players inside a certain sector, thus creating holes (spaces) between 2 players within the midfield or defensive line.

1.1 - HOW TO CREATE PASSING OPTIONS FOR THE BALL CARRIER

Following the fundamental premise explained on the previous page, it is important to train our players on how to build grids or appropriate passing options around the player in possession of the ball.

This should be done in such a way for this player to count on the following solutions (**see diagram below**):

1. **"Imbucata"** ("entry ball" with an accurate forward pass to a teammate - F in diagram)

2. **Lateral Support** (short sideways pass to the closest teammate - LCM in diagram)

3. **Front Support** (short forward pass to a supporting teammate - RCM in diagram)

4. **Back Support** (short backward pass to a supporting teammate - RB in diagram)

5. **Switch to Free Player** (switch the play with a long pass to a teammate free in space - LW in diagram)

6. **Pass Back** (pass back to reset - LCB in diagram)

EXAMPLE: Passing Options for the Defensive Midfielder

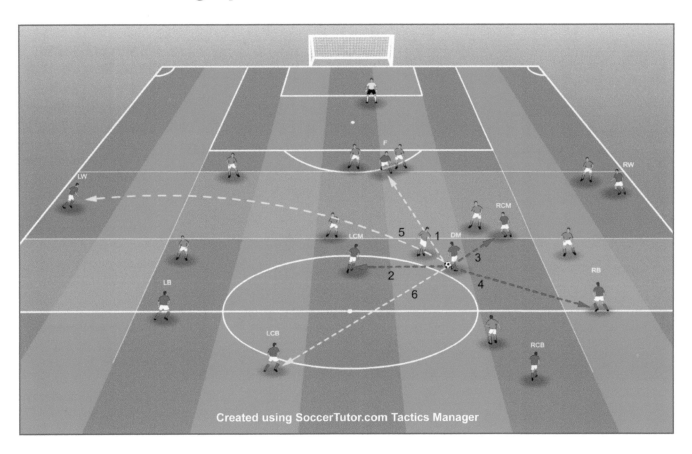

1.2 - PLAYING IN TACTICAL GRIDS: PASSING PATTERNS TO SWITCH THE PLAY

If the opposition are not particularly organised and aggressive, it's possible to simply switch play by passing inside to a player who then makes the pass across:

If the opposing team is well organised and does not allow this inside pass (close receiver is marked), it becomes important to know how to move the ball inside of the tactical grids.

The ball can be moved beyond the first support player (horizontally) with different sequences.

For each pattern we display, we have identified 2 possible developments on the weak side, with the attacking players establishing their positions and choosing the appropriate passing option, according to the tactical organisation of the opposition.

In the diagrams to follow, we show how to play through the opposing midfield and successfully switch the ball to the opposite flank.

The "Rhombus Shape" is clearly identifiable (on the side where the ball is), resulting from the players' specific positioning for the passing patterns to switch the play.

We use the example with the right back in possession. Here are 2 specific requirements:

1. Play beyond the closest teammate (RCM), who is in the middle of the rhombus shape and moves without the ball to open up a passing lane.

2. The forward (or advanced central midfielder) takes the position of "Front Support."

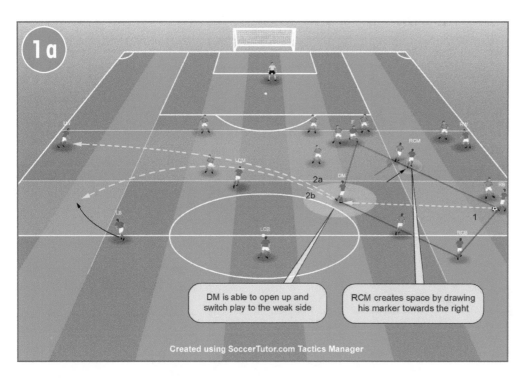

DM is able to open up and switch play to the weak side

RCM creates space by drawing his marker towards the right

Created using SoccerTutor.com Tactics Manager

CM Moves Wide to Create Space in the Centre for a Switch of Play to the Weak Side (1a):

This right back (RB) has the ball and the RCM is moving to the right side, thus "drawing" his marker with him and opening up a passing lane towards the defensive midfielder (DM).

The DM can then open the play up on the weak side by passing to the left back or left winger, both of whom are free in space.

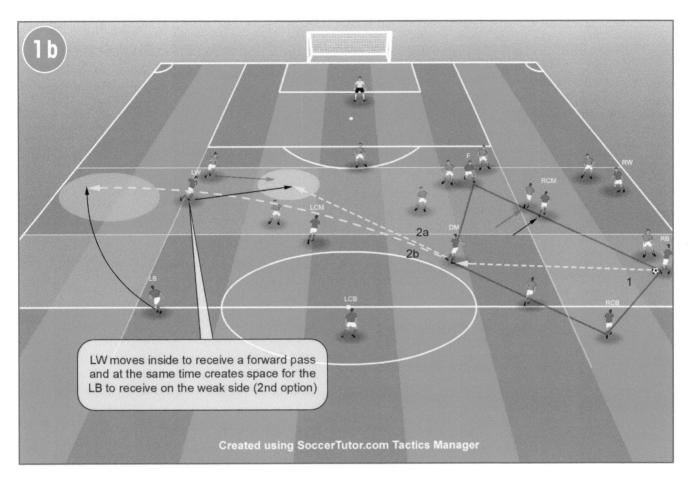

LW moves inside to receive a forward pass and at the same time creates space for the LB to receive on the weak side (2nd option)

Created using SoccerTutor.com Tactics Manager

CM Moves Wide to Create Space in the Centre for a Switch of Play to the Weak Side (1b):

This example is very similar to the previous one (1a). We just have a slightly different tactical situation on the weak side.

The winger (LW) moves inside to receive a forward pass in the centre and takes the opposition full back with him.

This movement allows the full back (LB) to move into a more advanced position to receive a switch of play high up the pitch.

This is a more advantageous situation than the previous example, with the left back receiving much closer to goal.

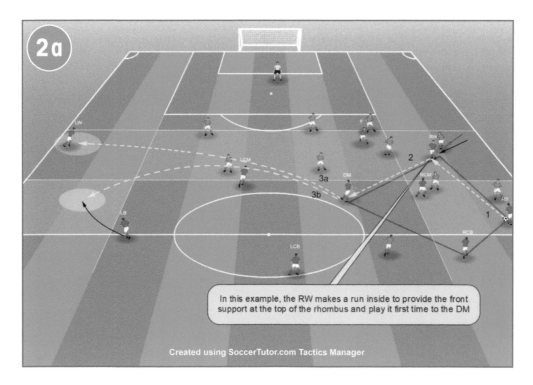

In this example, the RW makes a run inside to provide the front support at the top of the rhombus and play it first time to the DM

Created using SoccerTutor.com Tactics Manager

Using Winger as "Front Support" to Play into Centre for a Switch to the Weak Side (2a):

The RCM stays in position and is marked by his direct opponent. The RW moves inside and back to provide "Front Support" (top of rhombus).

The right back (RB) passes forward and the DM receives the ball indirectly via the right winger, who acts as a link player. He can then switch play to the left winger or left back.

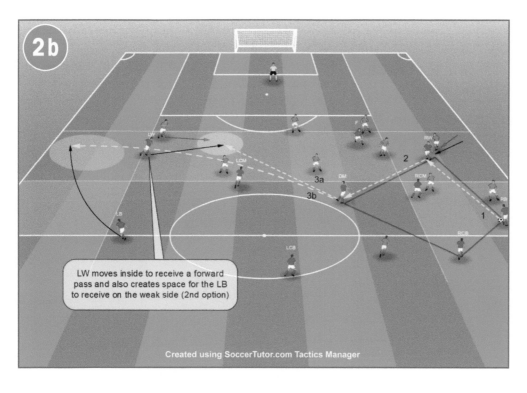

LW moves inside to receive a forward pass and also creates space for the LB to receive on the weak side (2nd option)

Created using SoccerTutor.com Tactics Manager

Using Winger as "Front Support" to Play into Centre for a Switch to the Weak Side (2b):

This example is very similar to the previous one (2a). We just have a slightly different tactical situation on the weak side.

The winger (LW) moves inside to receive a forward pass in the centre and takes the opposition full back with him.

This movement allows the full back (LB) to move into a more advanced position to receive a switch of play high up the pitch.

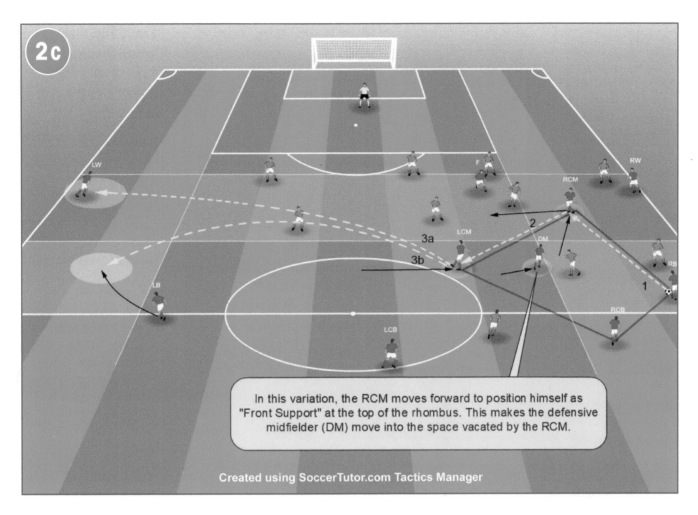

In this variation, the RCM moves forward to position himself as "Front Support" at the top of the rhombus. This makes the defensive midfielder (DM) move into the space vacated by the RCM.

Created using SoccerTutor.com Tactics Manager

RCM is "Front Support" and DM Moves Wide to Create Space for LCM to Receive and Switch Play:

The tactical examples on the previous page (2a & 2b) showed the winger (RW) moving into the position of "Front Support" at the top of the rhombus.

In this variation, the central midfielder (RCM) moves forward to position himself as "Front Support" at the top of the rhombus. This makes the defensive midfielder (DM) move into the space vacated by the RCM.

The right back (RB) passes forward to the RCM, who acts as the link player. This time the "Front Support" (RCM) player's pass is played into the centre to the left central midfielder (LCM), who has moved inside to receive. He can then switch play to the left winger (LW) or left back (LB).

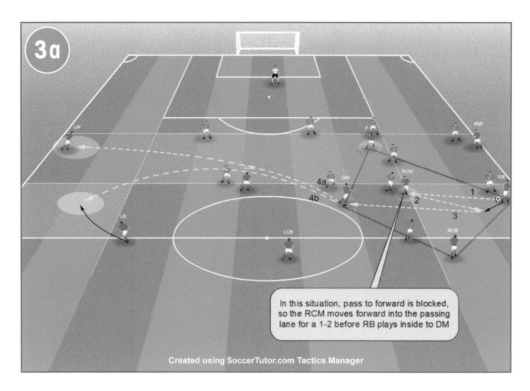

In this situation, pass to forward is blocked, so the RCM moves forward into the passing lane for a 1-2 before RB plays inside to DM

Created using SoccerTutor.com Tactics Manager

"Front Support" Option Blocked: Play I-2 with RCM, Pass to Centre and Switch Play (3a):

The forward is in the "Front Support" position but the passing lane to him is blocked by an opponent.

The right back plays a 1-2 with the RCM and moves slightly away from his marker to receive the return pass. The RCM moves forward a little to help open the passing lane for the right back to pass to the DM.

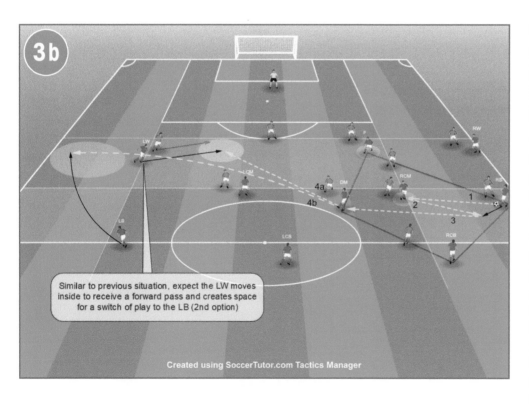

Similar to previous situation, expect the LW moves inside to receive a forward pass and creates space for a switch of play to the LB (2nd option)

Created using SoccerTutor.com Tactics Manager

"Front Support" Option Blocked: Play I-2 with RCM, Pass to Centre and Switch Play (3b):

This is very similar to 3a. We just have a slightly different tactical situation on the weak side.

The winger (LW) moves inside to receive a forward pass in the centre and takes the opposition full back with him. This movement also allows the full back (LB) to move into a more advanced position to receive a switch of play high up the pitch.

In this situation, the RCM moves to top of rhombus, opening up the passing lane for the DM (who is tightly maked) to play a 1-2 with the RB, before finding LCM who can switch the play.

Created using SoccerTutor.com Tactics Manager

RCM Moves to "Front Support": Play l-2 with DM, Pass into Centre for LCM Who Moves Inside and Switches Play:

In this tactical situation, we now have the right central midfielder (RCM) moving into the "Front Support" position (top of the rhombus).

In this example, the RCM has moved forward to take away an opponent and open the passing lane towards the defensive midfielder (DM). However, the DM is tightly marked by an opponent, so is unable to receive in space.

The right back (RB) therefore plays a 1-2 with the DM and moves slightly away from his marker to receive the return pass.

The DM moves forward to help open the passing lane for the right back (RB) to pass to the left central midfielder (LCM), who moves across to receive and then switches the play to the weak side.

Note how the midfielders make a rotation without the ball and switch positions according to the development of the pattern of play (this aspect will be explored further in the next section).

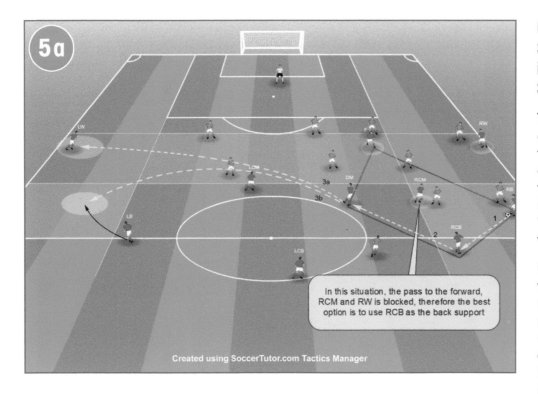

In this situation, the pass to the forward, RCM and RW is blocked, therefore the best option is to use RCB as the back support

Created using SoccerTutor.com Tactics Manager

Using RCB as "Back Support" to Play into the Centre for a Switch of Play (5a):

The "Front Support" option and the pass to the RCM are blocked by opponents. Therefore, the right back's (RB) best option is to use "Back Support" from the centre back (RCB).

Using this option is very effective, as the ball can be easily passed to the defensive midfielder (DM) via the centre back (RCB). The DM receives in space in the centre and can switch the play.

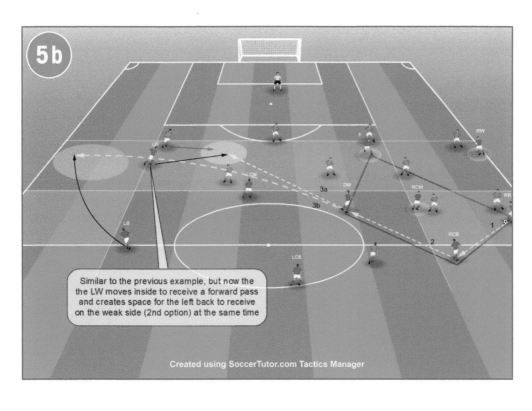

Similar to the previous example, but now the the LW moves inside to receive a forward pass and creates space for the left back to receive on the weak side (2nd option) at the same time

Created using SoccerTutor.com Tactics Manager

Using RCB as "Back Support" to Play into the Centre for a Switch of Play (5b):

This example is very similar to 5a. We just have a slightly different tactical situation on the weak side.

The winger (LW) moves inside to receive a forward pass in the centre and takes the opposition full back with him. This movement also allows the full back (LB) to move into a more advanced position to receive a switch of play high up the pitch.

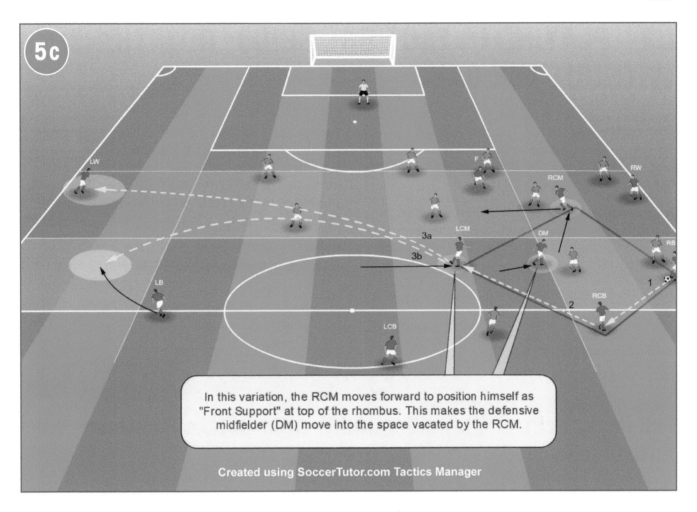

In this variation, the RCM moves forward to position himself as "Front Support" at top of the rhombus. This makes the defensive midfielder (DM) move into the space vacated by the RCM.

Created using SoccerTutor.com Tactics Manager

Using RCB as "Back Support" When DM Moves Wide to Create Space for LCM to Receive in the Centre and Switch Play:

In this tactical situation, we now have the right central midfielder (RCM) moving into the "Front Support" position (top of rhombus).

The defensive midfielder (DM) moves across into the RCM's position but the passing lane towards him is blocked by an opponent.

Therefore, the right back's best option is to use "Back Support" from the centre back (RCB).

As the defensive midfielder (DM) is occupying his marker, the left central midfielder (LCM) is able to move into the DM's position in the centre free in space.

Using this option is very effective, as the ball can be easily passed to the left central midfielder (LCM) via the centre back (RCB).

The LCM receives in space in the centre and can switch the play to the left back (LB) or the winger (LW).

1.3 - PLAYING IN TACTICAL GRIDS: ROTATIONS WITHOUT THE BALL

Through the types of build up play and ball possession that we have discussed, we must find the best timing and space for passing or dribbling the ball past the opposition's midfield line.

A very important aspect that teams must learn how to use, in order to "force" their opponents to move in specific directions (out of position), is based on **ROTATIONS**.

There are 2 different types of rotations:

1. Rotations **WITHOUT** the Ball

2. Rotations **WITH** the Ball

For rotations without the ball, 3 players exchange their positions in order to destabilise their opponent's defensive organisation. If this is done correctly, the ball carrier will most often then be presented with 1 or 2 potential receivers (options) for his pass.

In the following examples, we show some typical rotations to utilise when using the 4-3-3 formation.

Full Back, Central Midfielder and Winger Rotate Positions Anti-Clockwise (Centre Back in Possession)

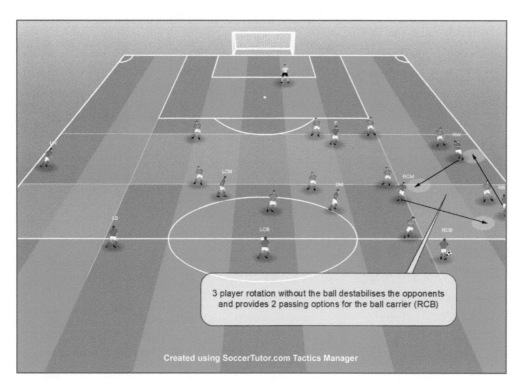

3 player rotation without the ball destabilises the opponents and provides 2 passing options for the ball carrier (RCB)

Created using SoccerTutor.com Tactics Manager

With the ball in possession of the centre back (RCB), the diagram shows how the right back (RB), right central midfielder (RCM) and right winger (RW) switch positions in an anti-clockwise rotation.

This movement should allow 1 or 2 of the players to get away from their marker and receive from the centre back.

This can be replicated in the exact same way on the left side of the pitch.

Full Back, Central Midfielder and Winger Rotate Positions Clockwise (Centre Back in Possession)

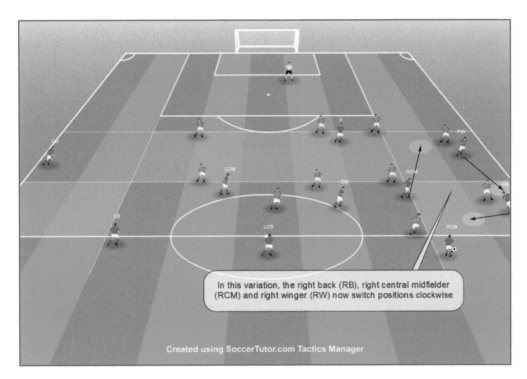

In this variation, the right back (RB), right central midfielder (RCM) and right winger (RW) now switch positions clockwise

Created using SoccerTutor.com Tactics Manager

This is a variation of the previous example, with the right back (RB), right central midfielder (RCM) and right winger (RW) now switching positions in a clockwise rotation.

Defensive Midfielder and Central Midfielders Rotate Positions (Centre Back in Possession)

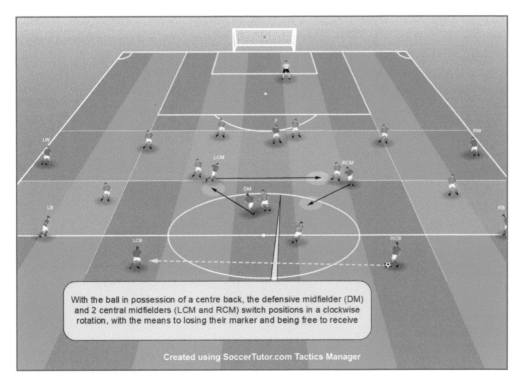

With the ball in possession of a centre back, the defensive midfielder (DM) and 2 central midfielders (LCM and RCM) switch positions in a clockwise rotation, with the means to losing their marker and being free to receive

Created using SoccerTutor.com Tactics Manager

With the ball in possession of a centre back, the diagram shows how the defensive midfielder (DM) and 2 central midfielders (LCM and RCM) switch positions in a clockwise rotation.

This movement should allow at least one of them to get away from their marker and receive from the centre back.

This can be replicated in the exact same way with an anti-clockwise rotation.

Central Midfielder, Winger and Forward Rotate Positions
(Full Back in Possession)

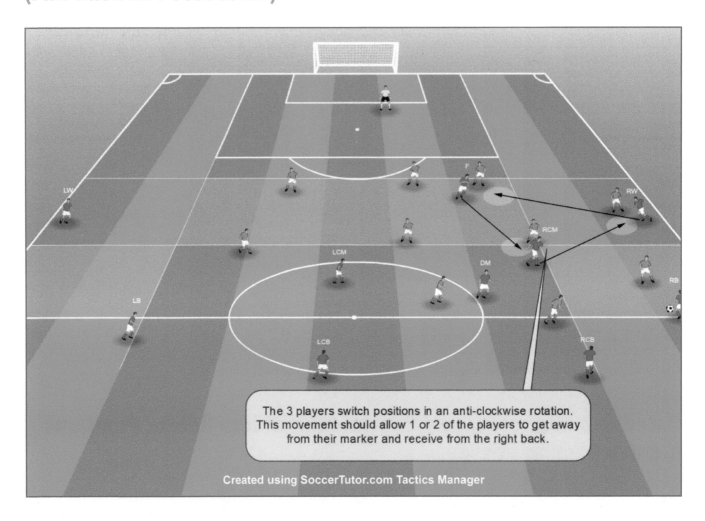

The 3 players switch positions in an anti-clockwise rotation. This movement should allow 1 or 2 of the players to get away from their marker and receive from the right back.

Created using SoccerTutor.com Tactics Manager

With the ball in possession of the right back (RB), the diagram shows how the right central midfielder (RCM), right winger (RW) and the forward (F) switch positions in an anti-clockwise rotation.

This movement should allow 1 or 2 of the players to get away from their marker and receive from the right back.

This can be replicated in the exact same way on the left side of the pitch.

1.4 - PLAYING IN TACTICAL GRIDS: ROTATIONS IN THE CENTRE WITH THE BALL

The rotations with the ball occur when the ball is already in possession of the 3 rotating players.

In this situation, the main purpose of the rotation, in addition to maintaining possession in a specific zone (usually in the centre of the pitch), is about:

1. **"Drawing" opposing players into that zone**

2. **And then moving the ball rapidly into an open space** (usually one of the flanks)

The following examples show a series of combinations between the defensive midfielder (DM) and 2 central midfielders (LCM and RCM). This involves a rapid ball exchange amongst themselves (one-touch passing), while rotating their positions at the same time.

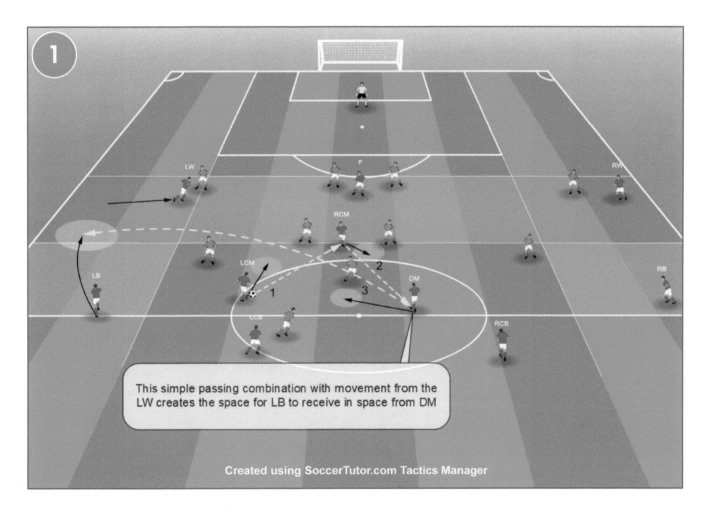

This simple passing combination with movement from the LW creates the space for LB to receive in space from DM

Example 1 is the simplest combination. The LCM passes to the RCM and he passes to the DM, as they all make rotating movements.

The DM is able to receive in space and pass out wide to the left back (LB).

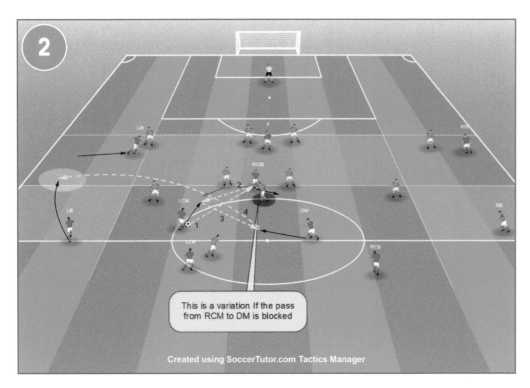

This is a variation If the pass from RCM to DM is blocked

Created using SoccerTutor.com Tactics Manager

In example 2, the LCM plays a 1-2 with the RCM and then simply passes back to the DM, as they all make rotating movements.

The DM is able to receive in space again and pass out wide to the left back (LB).

In this example, an extra pass (4th) is needed due to the positioning of the highlighted red player

Created using SoccerTutor.com Tactics Manager

In example 3, the LCM plays a 1-2 with the RCM and they both rotate, before the LCM plays it back to the RCM again.

The 4th pass is from the RCM to the DM who has moved across (part of rotation).

The DM is able to receive in space again and pass out wide to the left back (LB).

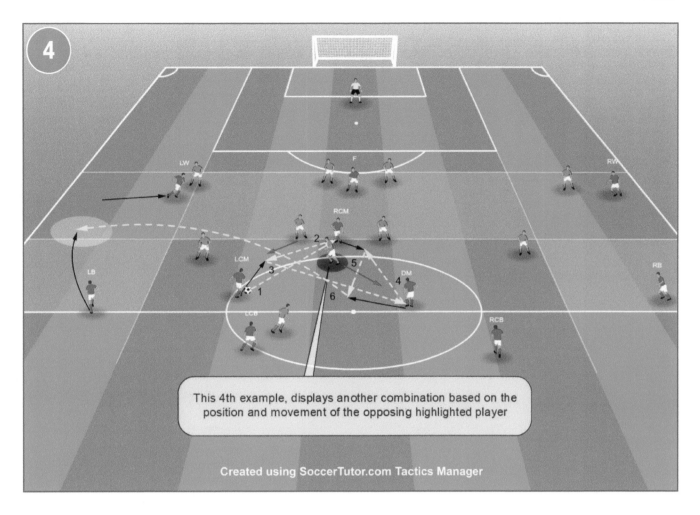

This 4th example, displays another combination based on the position and movement of the opposing highlighted player

Created using SoccerTutor.com Tactics Manager

In example 4, the LCM plays a 1-2 with the RCM and they both rotate. The LCM then passes across to the DM (3rd pass).

The DM then plays a 1-2 with the RCM (4th and 5th passes) and receives back after moving across as part of the rotational movement.

The DM is able to receive in space again and pass out wide to the left back (LB).

2. ACCELERATING THE ATTACK TO THE FINAL THIRD OF THE PITCH

2. ACCELERATING THE ATTACK TO THE FINAL THIRD OF THE PITCH

After creating the conditions for playing in between the opposition's midfield and defensive lines through ball movements and/or rotations, it is of fundamental importance to then accelerate the attack. This way, we can complete the "Creating Phase" and move forward to the "Finishing Phase."

"Accelerating the Attack" also signals a substantial change to our game. There is no more strategic movement of the ball, but instead we are now

attacking the opposition's defensive sector in the final third of the pitch. "Accelerating the Attack" consists of 3 parts:

2.1 - Creating an Opening (see previous section)

2.2 - "Imbucata" ("entry ball" with an accurate forward pass to a teammate)

2.3 - Dribbling the Ball Forward

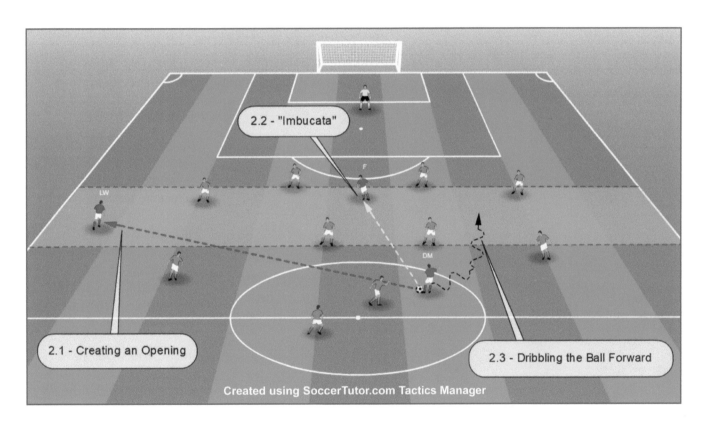

Created using SoccerTutor.com Tactics Manager

2.1 - CREATING AN OPENING

Creating an opening generally consists of passing the ball to a flank player (full back or winger).

We have already displayed this in the previous section, with a series of patterns of play. The objective is horizontal ball movement, followed by an opening toward the weak side.

Later, in the "Finishing Phase" chapter, we will show how these opening moves displayed can be utilised to then finish the attack and score.

2.2 – "IMBUCATA" (ENTRY BALL)

Another approach to move the ball in behind the opposition's midfield line is to use the "imbucata." This pass is usually, but not exclusively, on the ground. This pass enables us to connect with the forward who can receive with his back to goal (examples 1 & 4), the winger cutting inside to receive between the lines as he is running, or a central midfielder who has moved forward and in between the lines (examples 2 & 3).

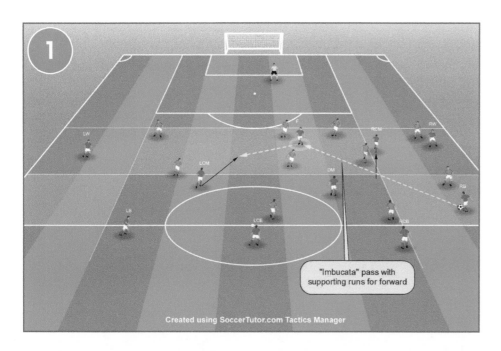

"Imbucata" pass with supporting runs for forward

Created using SoccerTutor.com Tactics Manager

"Imbucata" to the Forward with Back to Goal:

This example shows an "imbucata" pass through the centre with the forward's back to goal - from this point he needs support players to lay the ball back or play in behind to.

We can also have a similar example with the winger moving inside off the flank to receive between the lines (either with back to goal or with space to turn).

RCM moves forward in between the lines

Created using SoccerTutor.com Tactics Manager

"Imbucata" to Central Midfielder with Time and Space to Turn:

The RCM receives an "imbucata" in behind the midfield line with time and space to turn, move forward and attempt to finish the attack.

If the RCM decides to pass the ball back instead of turning and developing the finishing touches of the attack, the effectiveness of the move will be jeopardised.

"Imbucata" to Central Midfielder with Back to Goal:

This is similar to example 2, but now the RCM is marked by an opponent and unable to turn. He instead acts as a "link player" and simply plays the ball back to a free teammate (DM).

If the RCM receives and tries to turn in this situation, he would more than likely lose possession for his team.

Central Midfielder Provides Support to Forward Who Receives "Imbucata":

If there is an "imbucata" pass to the forward, he needs support. In this example, the RCM moves forward between the lines to receive the lay-off. He then plays the ball in behind (1-2 combination) for the forward to finish the attack.

If players did not support the forward (RCM in this example), possession would most likely be lost.

2.3 – DRIBBLING THE BALL FORWARD

Another way to move the ball beyond the opposition's midfield line is with an individual player dribbling the ball forward. This player may be able to dribble the ball up to the area in front of the opponent's defensive line, therefore creating a position to enter the finishing phase.

Even this approach, as the previous ones discussed, requires the team as a whole to create the conditions to "open/expand" the distances

between the opposing midfielders, thus helping the individual effort of dribbling through the lines in possession of the ball.

This can be done by a midfielder or winger in central areas or on one of the flanks.

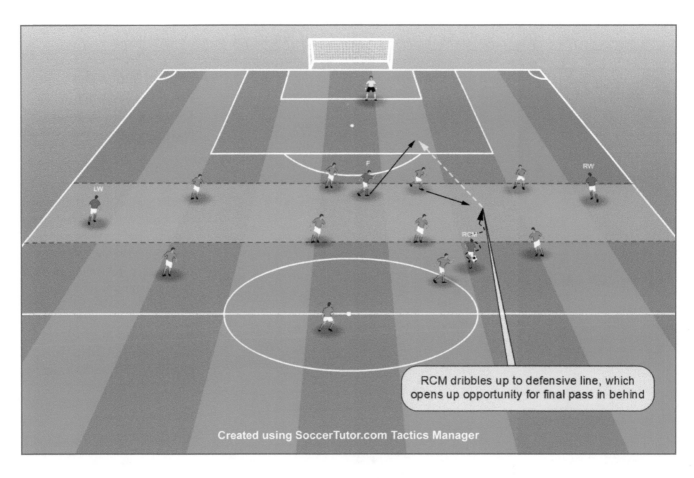

RCM dribbles up to defensive line, which opens up opportunity for final pass in behind

Created using SoccerTutor.com Tactics Manager

If the acceleration of this move (dribbling forward) does not result in the team entering the finishing phase, it is important to maintain possession of the ball and come back to the creating process.

We don't want to force the play to try to get through the opposition's defensive line, unless there is an opening and adequate chance of success.

CREATING AN OPENING AND ACCELERATING THE ATTACK: CONCLUSION

On the basis of what we have discussed in this chapter, the essential points that a coach has to analyse are:

1. CREATING AN OPENING

- How to maintain possession and create the conditions/openings to move the ball beyond the opposing midfield line and in front of their defensive line (switching play to the weak side).

- How to utilise the rhombus shape to coordinate the positioning of players deployed in different lines (defence, midfield, attack) and how to manage possession of the ball.

- How and when to utilise sideways, forward, diagonal or backward ball movements.

- How and when to utilise rotations of players.

- How to optimise patterns of play in relation to the opponent's tactical organisation/shape.

2. ACCELERATING THE ATTACK

- How to accelerate an attack after playing between the lines, leading to a goal.

- How to create an opening, most often to the weak side flank.

- How to exploit the situation after an "imbucata" (forward entry ball).

- How to exploit the situation after a player dribbles forward to break through the lines.

KEY POINT:

All this is a prelude to Chapter 5 and "The Finishing Phase," where we examine the playing options when the ball is in behind the opposition's midfield line and in front of the defensive line (in the final third).

In particular, we focus on playing in behind the defensive line and into the penalty area (final pass) to try and score a goal. In the finishing phase, the combinations we use are between 2-3 players.

PRACTICE EXAMPLES FOR THE CREATING PHASE

I. Pass to the Forward and Retain Possession in an 8 v 5 Positional Practice

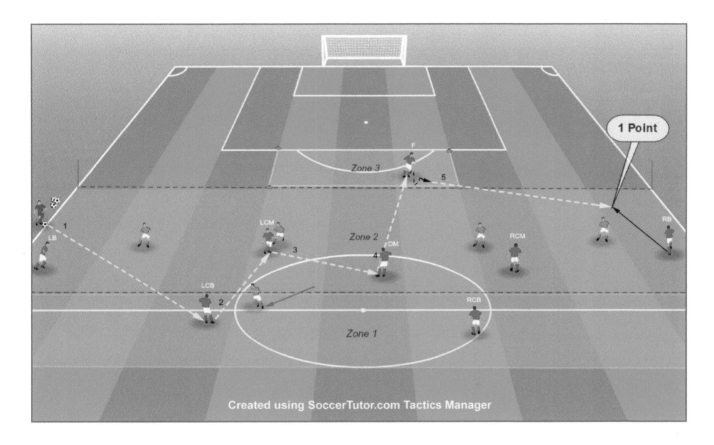

Attacking Objective: Pass into free space for the forward + retain possession.

Defending Objective: Recover the ball and start a counter attack.

Practice Description

Using the area shown, we mark out 3 zones. In zone 1, we have 2 blue centre backs. In zone 2, we have 3 central midfielders and 2 full backs. In the smaller zone 3, we have 1 forward who wants to receive a forward pass. All blue players stay within their zones throughout.

The red team have 4 midfielders and 1 forward - they can move freely across zones 1 and 2.

1. The practice starts with the coach's pass to a centre back.

2. The blue team have to move the ball and find open spaces/lines to pass to the forward. The forward must receive a pass within zone 3 and play the ball back to a teammate successfully (1 point).

3. The blue team retain possession, play back to a centre back and the practice continues with the same aim.

4. If the red team win the ball, they try to dribble the ball past the end line (1 point) - if this happens, the teams switch roles and we restart the practice.

Coaching Point: The forward must be always moving, trying to open up a passing line to receive.

2. Possession and Attacking in Behind in a 7 v 7 (+3) Dynamic Game

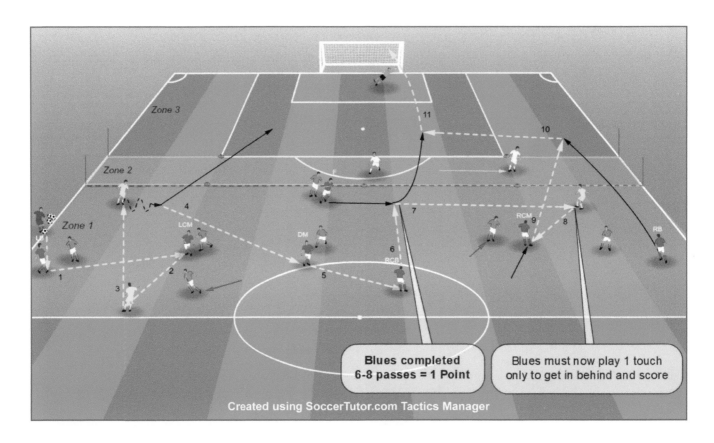

Blues completed 6-8 passes = 1 Point

Blues must now play 1 touch only to get in behind and score

Created using SoccerTutor.com Tactics Manager

Attacking Objective: Ball possession and attacking in behind the opposition.

Defending Objective: Collective pressing, interceptions, winning the ball and transition play.

Practice Description

Using the area shown, the pitch is divided into 3 zones. In zone 1, we have 7 v 7 + 3 yellow neutral players (centre back and 2 wingers) who play with the team in possession. Both teams are organised into a 4-3-3 formation but you can adapt the red team to your next opponents.

1. The practice starts with the coach's pass to one team who therefore become the attacking team (blues in diagram). They have a 10 v 7 numerical advantage in the main zone with the neutral players.

2. The first aim for the attacking team (blues) is to complete 6-8 passes (1 point) before they are able to play out of zone 1.

3. The blues can then leave zone 1 with the second aim to attack using 1 touch passes and score a goal, while trying to avoid the 2 white defenders (who must stay within zone 2).

4. If the blues finish their attack, score or the ball goes out of play, the practice starts with the coach's pass to the reds and the team roles reversed. Both teams attack, in alternate fashion, in the same direction.

5. If the defending team (reds) win the ball, the practice continues with the team roles reversed. After winning the ball, the reds would have to complete 6-8 passes (1 point) before they can attack the goal with 1 touch passes.

3. Playing Through the Centre in a Zonal Tactical Practice

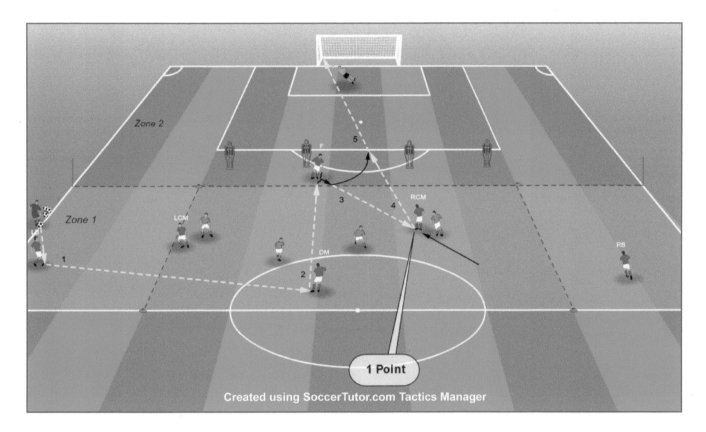

Created using SoccerTutor.com Tactics Manager

Attacking Objective: Ball circulation (exploiting width), forward passing (exploiting depth) and finishing through central areas.

Defending Objective: Ball recovery and transition from defence to attack (dribbling past the halfway line with the ball).

Practice Description

Using half a pitch, we divide the area into 2 zones. The blue attacking team have 2 full backs (in separate side zones) and 3 central midfielders in zone 1 and 1 forward in zone 2. The red defending team have 4 midfielders in the central part of zone 1 and there are also 4 mannequins (defenders) in zone 2.

1. The practice starts with the coach's pass and the blue attacking team have to move the ball and find open spaces/lanes to pass to the forward in zone 2, who can move horizontally, but not towards the flanks.

2. The forward has to take up an effective position behind the red team's midfielders, receive/control the ball and pass it back to one of his teammates (1 point).

3. The blue team attack through the central area to try and score a goal (1 point). The red players can track back to defend their goal. If the blues score, the practice restarts with the same objectives.

4. If the red team win the ball at any time, they then make a fast transition from defence to attack. Their aim is to dribble the ball past the halfway line (1 point).

4. Ball Circulation to Exploit Wide Areas in an 8 v 4 Zonal Tactical Practice

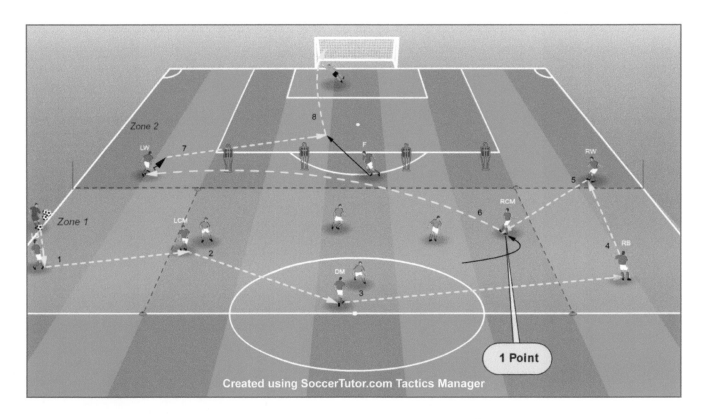

Attacking Objective: Ball circulation (exploiting width), forward passing (exploiting depth) and finishing through specific combinations/patterns of play.

Defending Objective: Ball recovery and transition from defence to attack (dribbling past the halfway line with the ball).

Practice Description

Using the same set up as the previous practice, we now add 2 wingers for the blue team who start in zone 2 with the forward.

1. The practice starts with the coach's pass and the blue attacking team have to move the ball and find open spaces/lanes to pass to either winger or the forward in zone 2 (emphasis on width with wingers).

2. A forward or winger has to take up an effective position behind the red team's midfielders, receive/control the ball and pass it back to one of his teammates (1 point).

3. From this point, the blue team attack and try and score a goal (1 point) using one of these combinations:

   • Pass to the furthest winger (LW in diagram example) who can then pass into the box for the forward.

   • Pass to the forward, who lays the ball off for an oncoming midfielder. The team can then either play through the centre or via the flanks to finish the attack.

4. If the red team win the ball at any time, they then make a fast transition from defence to attack. Their aim is to dribble the ball past the halfway line (1 point).

5. Ball Circulation to Exploit Wide Areas in a 10 v 6 Zonal Tactical Practice

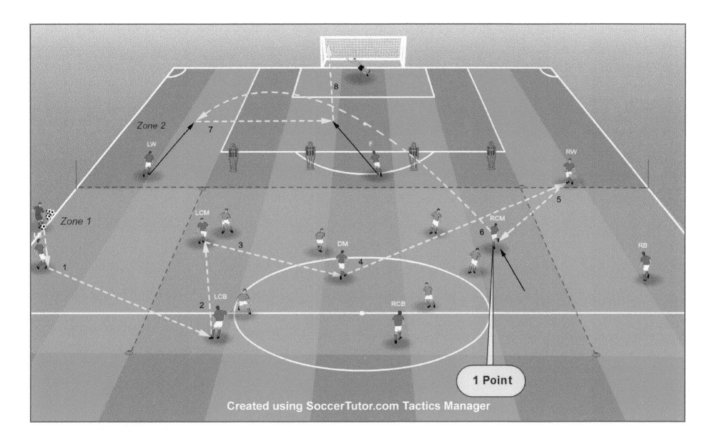

Attacking and Defending Objectives: The same as the previous practice.

Practice Description

Using the same set up as the previous practice, we now add 2 blue centre backs and 2 red forwards. In the diagram example, the red defending team are in a 4-4-2 formation - you can adapt this to the formation of the next opponents i.e. 4-3-3, 4-5-1, 4-2-3-1, 3-5-2 etc.

1. The practice starts with the coach's pass and the blue attacking team have to move the ball and find open spaces/lanes to pass to either winger or the forward in zone 2.

2. A forward or winger has to take up an effective position behind the red team's midfielders, receive/control the ball and pass it back to one of his teammates (1 point).

3. From this point, the blue team attack and try and score a goal (1 point) using one of these combinations:

   • Pass to the furthest winger (LW in diagram example), who can then pass into the box for the forward (the pass from the full back to the winger is not allowed).

   • Pass to the forward, who lays the ball off for an oncoming midfielder. The team can then either play through the centre or via the flanks to finish the attack.

4. If the red team win the ball at any time, they then make a fast transition from defence to attack. Their aim is to dribble the ball past the halfway line (1 point).

6. Ball Circulation, Switching Play and Attacking Combinations in a 10 v 11 Game

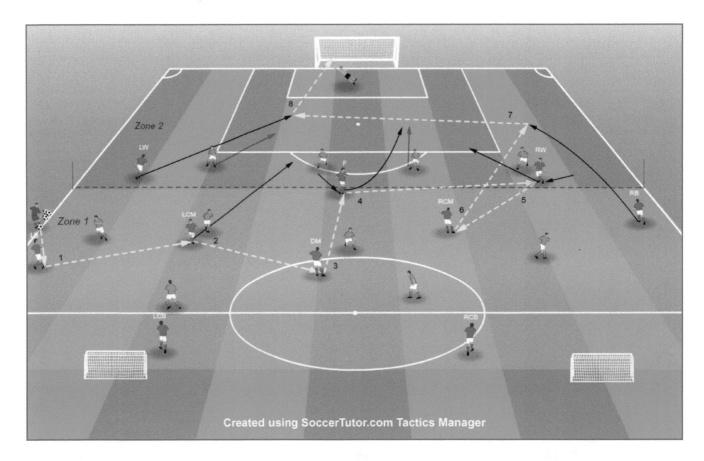

Attacking Objective: Ball circulation (exploiting width), forward passing (exploiting depth) and finishing with freedom of decision making.

Practice Description

Using the same set up as the previous practice, we now simply add 4 active red defenders. Now when the blue team are trying to finish their attack, they will be fully contested.

In the diagram example, the red defending team are in a 4-4-2 formation - you can adapt this to the formation of the next opponents i.e. 4-3-3, 4-5-1, 4-2-3-1, 3-5-2 etc.

The players are now free to make their own decisions for which combinations to use - see the previous practices in this section and the diagram above for good examples.

CHAPTER 5

THE FINISHING PHASE

THE FINISHING PHASE

The objectives of "The Finishing Phase" are to penetrate the opposition's defence, play a final pass and finish.

To create the conditions to shoot at goal, we have 3 options:

1. Move the ball around the opposition's defence and attack from the flanks.

2. Break through the opposition's defence with a final pass (assist) or by dribbling forward through the centre of the pitch.

3. Move toward the goal and shoot from outside the penalty area. It is important that the player has a high level of technical skill for long distance shooting.

In conclusion, "The Finishing Phase" has 3 different ways to finish an attack:

1. **WIDE ATTACK (CROSSING)**

2. **THROUGH BALL**

3. **SHOT FROM OUTSIDE THE PENALTY AREA**

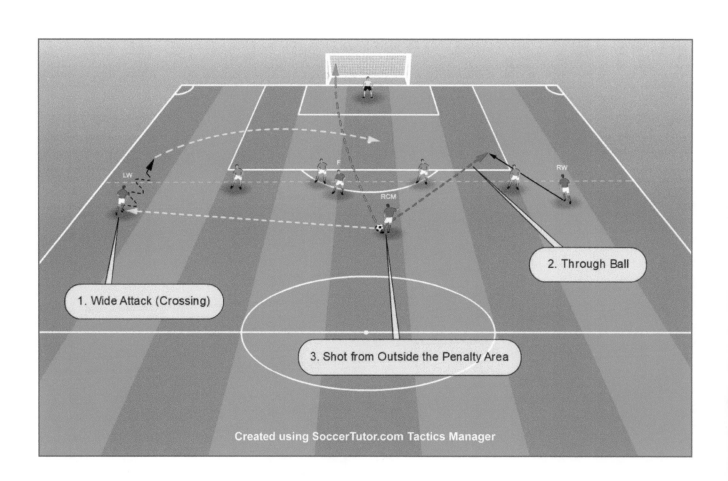

1. Wide Attack (Crossing)

2. Through Ball

3. Shot from Outside the Penalty Area

Created using SoccerTutor.com Tactics Manager

CONDITIONS AND SITUATIONS FOR FINISHING AN ATTACK (CREATING AN OPEN BALL SITUATION)

During the finishing phase, we can utilise the following types of passes (assists):

- **CROSS** (driven or floated)

- **THROUGH BALL** (on the ground or in the air)

- **WALL / REBOUND** (one-touch deflecting pass)

Before analysing some of the possible attacking moves with the 4-3-3 system, let's identify principles and conditions that must be met in order to finalise the attacking move.

The attacking phase is completed with a shot that can derive from:

1. An individual effort.

2. An assist from the player in possession of the ball to a teammate who shoots on goal.

3. Intercepting a "lost ball" in the penalty area (passing error of an opponent, favourable bounce of the ball or deflection off an opponent).

In order for the player in possession of the ball to complete an "assist" pass for a teammate, the following conditions are needed:

- **OPEN BALL SITUATION:** The pressure on the player in possession should not make it difficult to play the ball.

- The receiver of the pass is in the right conditions (in terms of distance from goal, from the teammate and from the direct opponent) to control the ball and then shoot on goal.

OPEN BALL SITUATIONS

As mentioned above, an "open ball situation" is when the player in possession of the ball is not pressed by opponents who could delay or intercept his pass at the outset, and who is therefore in a good position for passing the ball to a teammate.

An "open ball situation" can either be a:

- **GENERAL OPEN BALL SITUATION:**
  The "general open ball situation" reflects the situation of players positioned at a considerable distance away from the opposition's goal, therefore not likely to provide an assist for their forwards.

- **OPEN BALL SITUATION FOR A FINAL PASS:**
  An "open ball situation for a final pass" reflects the situation of a player who, without immediate pressure from an opponent, due to limited distance and possible quick execution time, can effectively assist the ball to a teammate for a shot on goal.

The "Open Ball Situation for a Final Pass" can occur with the assisting player in 2 different contexts:

- **FRONTAL:** Corresponds in general to a through pass (leading pass in behind defensive line) for a teammate moving toward the goal.

- **BACK TO GOAL:** The open ball situation with back to goal is the classic deflecting touch for a teammate moving into open space, or a lay-off pass for a teammate coming from behind.

For the finishing phase to be successful, we want the following 3 conditions to be met:

1. Potential to attack the opposition's defence and defensive line.

2. Freedom of play on the part of the player in possession of the ball.

3. Optimal movements of the attacking players (in terms of timing and direction of play) to get away from their markers to finish attacks.

All 3 of these parameters have to be in place to carry out the finishing phase as planned, otherwise the players have to resort to alternate moves/patterns.

THE FINISHING PHASE: TACTICAL CONTEXTS

OPPOSITION DEFENCE MOVE BACK WHEN THERE IS SPACE IN BEHIND

A player in possession of the ball with an open ball situation and very close to the opposition's defensive line is not always able to carry out the finishing phase.

If the opponents have space behind them, most likely they will move back collectively, to avoid the consequences of a through pass from the attacking team. This means that the correct defensive movement of the opponent's defensive sector can make it near possible for the forwards to receive a through pass.

In these situations, the forwards should follow these tactical instructions:

1. Initially move forward with the opposing defenders, in order to force them to withdraw as much as possible.

2. Be prepared to receive a pass in front of the opposing defensive line when they move back, very close to their penalty area. This is especially important if an opponent moves to put pressure on the teammate who is in possession of the ball - move to receive before he is no longer able to play the pass.

3. Receive the pass and be ready to play a through ball to a teammate running in behind the defensive line, or be ready to shoot at goal.

PLAYER IN POSSESSION IS CLOSE TO THE OPPOSITION'S DEFENSIVE LINE WITH A CLOSED BALL SITUATION

This can happen if the high pressure of the direct opponent or the distance from the potential receiver stops the possibility of carrying out the finishing phase, thus creating a closed ball situation.

In these situations, the teammates of the player in possession of the ball (potential receivers) don't move to receive the ball in behind, but try to instead focus on maintaining possession for their team.

Specifically, the potential receiver will have to:

- Get close to the player in possession.

- Execute an exchange (or 1-2 combination) with the player in possession, in order to convert the closed ball situation into an open ball situation.

- Read the tactical situation and optimise the next moves in relation to the new playing context and start a new attack.

HOW TO CREATE AN OPEN BALL SITUATION

The various methods for creating an "Open Ball Situation for a Final Pass" and those for converting a closed ball situation into an open ball situation are as follows:

1. **DRIBBLING:** The player in possession of the ball beats his direct opponent and has time and space to carry out the finishing touch (or any other technical move).

2. **COMBINATION PLAY:** Following a "give and go" or "give and follow" combination, the ball carrier can take out the direct opponent.

3. **"IMBUCATA" (ENTRY BALL):** Vertical pass for a player (usually with back to goal) positioned near the opposing defensive sector. In this situation, the player can use a deflecting touch for a teammate moving into open space, or a lay-off pass for a teammate coming from behind.

4. **DIAGONAL THROUGH BALL:** Diagonal pass for a teammate (generally facing the goal) near the opposing defensive sector, who, thanks to this pass, now has available space in front to play a final pass in behind.

5. **LAY-OFF PASS:** Pass toward a player in a supporting position (facing the opposing goal), positioned between the lines and able to feed teammates who make cutting runs towards the goal.

I. CREATING CHANCES IN THE FINAL THIRD

I. CREATING CHANCES IN THE FINAL THIRD

In this section, we display 5 different tactical situations, with the aim to create chances in the final third:

1.1 - Attacking Options for the Full Back High Up the Flank

1.2 - Attacking Options for the Central Midfielder in the Middle of the Pitch

1.3 - Attacking Options for the Winger on the Flank

1.4 - Attacking Options When the Winger Moves Inside to Receive Between the Lines

1.5 - Attacking Options when the Forward Receives an "Imbucata" (Vertical) Pass

These attacking options can be finished in the 3 following ways:

1. **WIDE ATTACKS** (Attacking wide, around the opposition's defensive unit)

2. **THROUGH BALL** (Passing in behind the defensive line)

3. **SHOT FROM OUTSIDE THE PENALTY AREA** (Shooting from long distance)

* In the next section "2. OPTIONS BLOCKED: MAINTAIN POSSESSION AND START NEW ATTACK," we will explain an alternative situation when the above options are blocked.

If this happens, the aim changes to playing the ball back, maintaining possession and then starting a new attack.

1.1 - ATTACKING OPTIONS FOR THE FULL BACK HIGH UP THE FLANK

Following combination play in the midfield zone, the full back receives the ball near the sideline. At this point, he must have an order of priority to continue the attacking move. We display 5 different options:

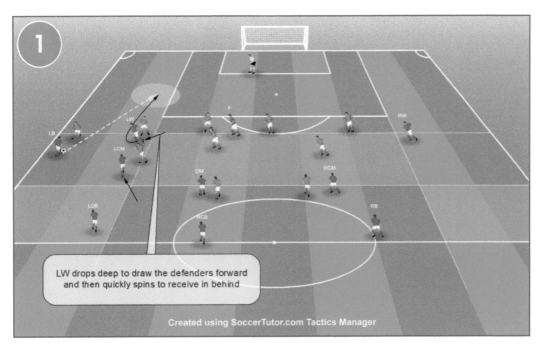

LW drops deep to draw the defenders forward and then quickly spins to receive in behind

Created using SoccerTutor.com Tactics Manager

Through Ball in Behind:

This example shows the winger (LW) checking away from a marker and moving to receive in behind.

Other options (when conditions are right) include passing to the forward (F) or central midfielder (LCM) if they make runs into the open space.

If the direct assist is not on (blocked by the opposing Right Back), another option is a quick 1-2 for the LB to receive in behind

Created using SoccerTutor.com Tactics Manager

1-2 with Winger + Receive in Behind:

If the option of a direct assist is not there, the left back must evaluate whether he can attack the space in behind himself, via a combination with a teammate.

This example shows a 1-2 with the winger (LW).

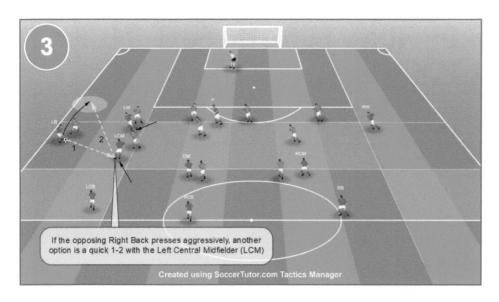

If the opposing Right Back presses aggressively, another option is a quick 1-2 with the Left Central Midfielder (LCM)

Created using SoccerTutor.com Tactics Manager

1-2 with CM + Receive in Behind:

This example is a variation of the previous one and shows a 1-2 with the central midfielder (LCM).

The full back is able to receive the pass back high up the pitch and in behind the defensive line.

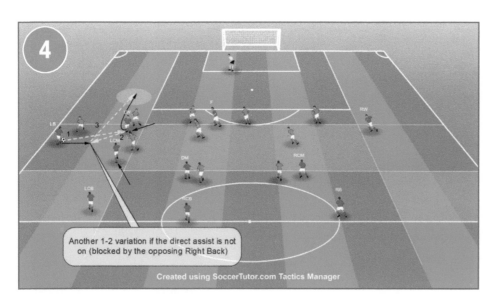

Another 1-2 variation if the direct assist is not on (blocked by the opposing Right Back)

Created using SoccerTutor.com Tactics Manager

1-2 with Winger + Pass in Behind for Winger:

Another alternative is to play a 1-2 combination and then follow that with a through pass in behind for that same player.

This diagram shows an example of this option with the winger (LW).

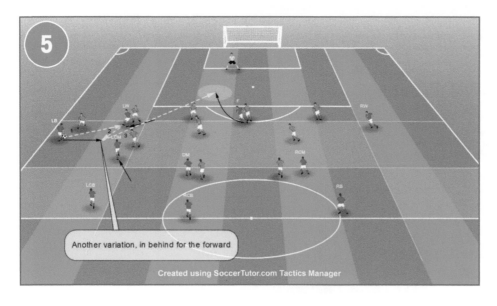

Another variation, in behind for the forward

Created using SoccerTutor.com Tactics Manager

1-2 with Closest Teammate + Pass in Behind for Third Player:

Another possibility includes a 1-2 with a nearby teammate (LW in diagram), followed by a through pass to another teammate.

This diagram example shows a 1-2 with the winger (LW), followed by a through ball to the forward (F) in the box.

OPTIONS BLOCKED: FULL BACK PLAYS AN "IMBUCATA" (ENTRY BALL) INSIDE TO FORWARD

If the possibilities of a direct assist and a combination with a nearby teammate are both blocked, a viable option could be an "imbucata" (entry ball) for an advanced teammate. In our examples, this is an inside pass to the forward. This tactical situation can lead to several developments, as shown in the following 5 diagrams:

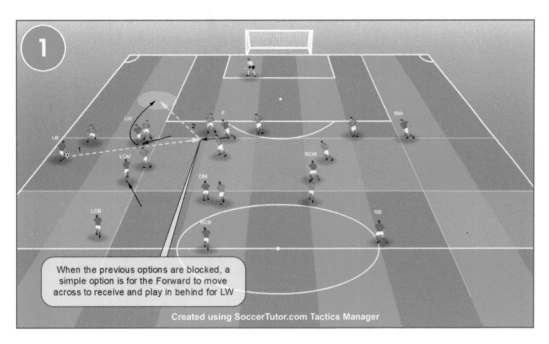

Forward Plays a First Time Pass to the Winger in Behind:

The left back's (LB) 2 closest passing options blocked.

The forward reacts and moves across to provide a good option and quickly play in behind.

> When the previous options are blocked, a simple option is for the Forward to move across to receive and play in behind for LW

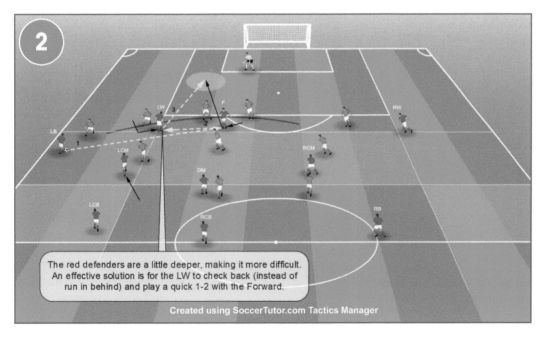

Forward Plays 1-2 with Winger to Receive in the Box:

As the red defence is deeper and the LW is not tightly marked, the previous example wouldn't be as effective.

The LW creates space by checking back to receive and the blues just have to play 1 more pass to get in behind.

> The red defenders are a little deeper, making it more difficult. An effective solution is for the LW to check back (instead of run in behind) and play a quick 1-2 with the Forward.

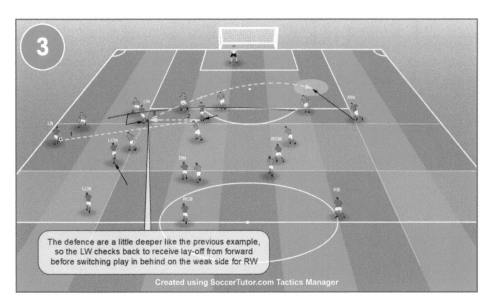

The defence are a little deeper like the previous example, so the LW checks back to receive lay-off from forward before switching play in behind on the weak side for RW

Created using SoccerTutor.com Tactics Manager

Forward's Lay-Off to Winger Who Passes to Opposite Winger:

As the red defence is deeper again, the LW creates space by checking back to receive.

In this variation, he plays an aerial pass to the RW in behind on the opposite side.

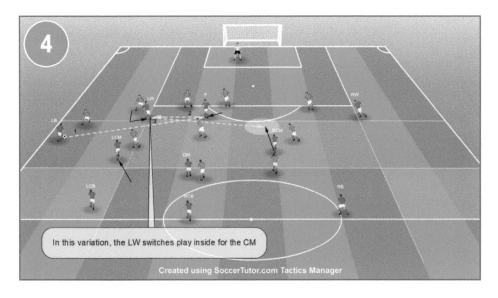

In this variation, the LW switches play inside for the CM

Created using SoccerTutor.com Tactics Manager

Forward's Lay-Off to Winger Who Passes Inside for CM:

In this variation of the previous example, the RCM makes a forward run to receive in space in the centre - he can either shoot from outside the penalty area or play a through ball in behind for a teammate (forward or RW).

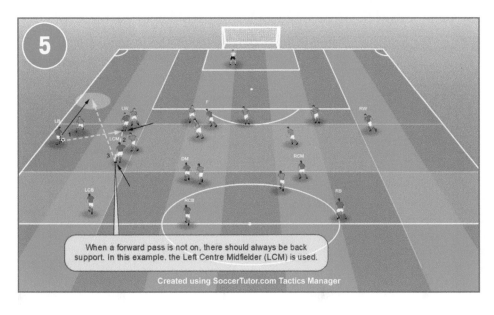

When a forward pass is not on, there should always be back support. In this example, the Left Centre Midfielder (LCM) is used.

Created using SoccerTutor.com Tactics Manager

Winger's Lay-Off to CM Who Passes in Behind for Full Back:

When there is a lack of front support options, there is always the option of playing back to a free player who can then play in behind (open ball situation).

In this example, the LB is able to make a well timed run in behind to receive.

I.2 - ATTACKING OPTIONS FOR THE CENTRAL MIDFIELDER IN THE MIDDLE OF THE PITCH

The central midfielder can advance beyond the opposition's midfield line and receive a vertical pass ("imbucata") there or, through individual dribbling, move up to the opposing defensive line, thus creating a situation where his team can finish the attacking phase.

The tactical solutions available to this midfielder are similar to that of the full back which we have already shown, with some differences:

1. Direct assist (through ball) for a teammate's run in behind

2. Play a 1-2 combination to receive in behind (and in the box)

3. Play a 1-2 combination + pass to a third player in behind

4. Combination play with 2 teammates + receiving in behind yourself

The following 7 diagrams show these possibilities involving the central midfielder (RCM).

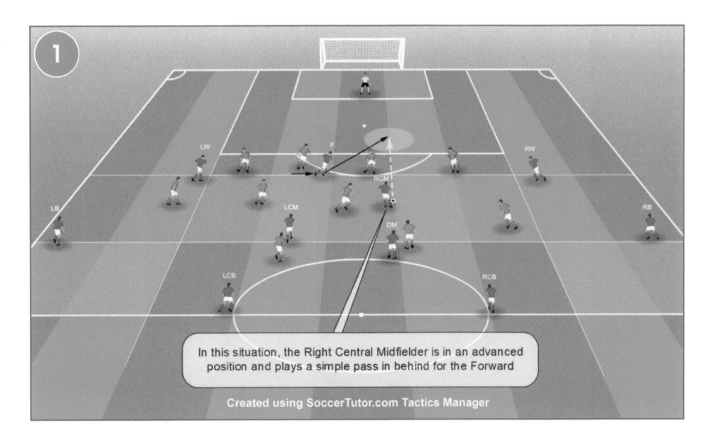

In this situation, the Right Central Midfielder is in an advanced position and plays a simple pass in behind for the Forward

Created using SoccerTutor.com Tactics Manager

Through Pass in Behind for Forward:

There is an open ball situation with no pressure on the ball, so the RCM can simply play in behind for the forward.

In this example, a diagonal pass in behind for the RW

Created using SoccerTutor.com Tactics Manager

Through Pass in Behind for Winger:

As in the previous example, there is an open ball situation with no pressure on the ball.

This variation shows the RCM playing a simple ball between the centre back and full back, in behind for the RW.

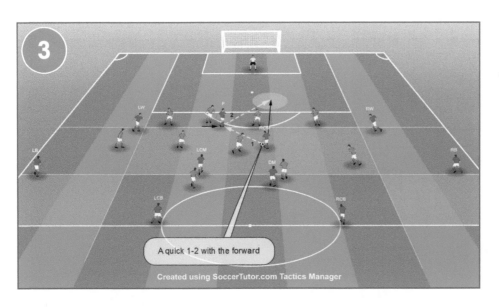

A quick 1-2 with the forward

Created using SoccerTutor.com Tactics Manager

1-2 with Forward + Receive in the Box:

This time there is more pressure on the ball from an opponent, so the RCM plays a quick 1-2, makes a forward run and receives in behind.

In this situation, the positioning of the defenders is staggered, which opens up space in behind

Created using SoccerTutor.com Tactics Manager

1-2 with Winger + Receive in the Box:

The opposing centre back is in a more advanced position which leaves a gap in the defensive line, so a quick 1-2 with the winger is used to exploit the space and receive in behind again.

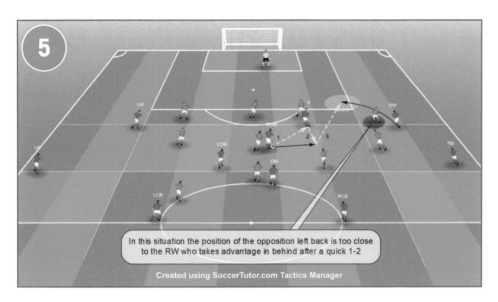

In this situation the position of the opposition left back is too close to the RW who takes advantage in behind after a quick 1-2

Created using SoccerTutor.com Tactics Manager

1-2 with Closest Teammate + Pass in Behind:

The forward is tightly marked and the opposing red left back is further forward than the other defenders.

A lay-off and pass in behind for the RW is by far the best solution here.

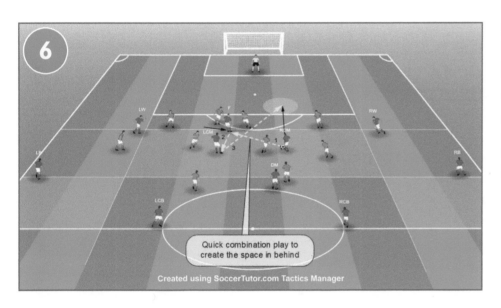

Quick combination play to create the space in behind

Created using SoccerTutor.com Tactics Manager

Combination Play with 2 Teammates to Receive in Behind (1):

The pass to the forward attracts the opposition's left centre back, which creates a gap for our RCM to receive in behind.

If the Red Left Back is in a balanced position, the winger (RW) moves inside to provide a simple passing option

Created using SoccerTutor.com Tactics Manager

Combination Play with 2 Teammates to Receive in Behind (2):

This time, there is no gap in the opposition defence, so the winger (RW) moves inside to create space to receive.

The RW also creates an angle to pass in behind for the RCM, who makes a well-timed run into the box.

I.3 - ATTACKING OPTIONS FOR THE WINGER ON THE FLANK

As already seen with the tactical examples for the full back and central midfielder, the priority for the player in possession is to pass to a teammate who runs in behind (free space in front of him) and, as a second option, develop effective combinations with nearby teammates.

The Winger's Options for a Direct Through Pass

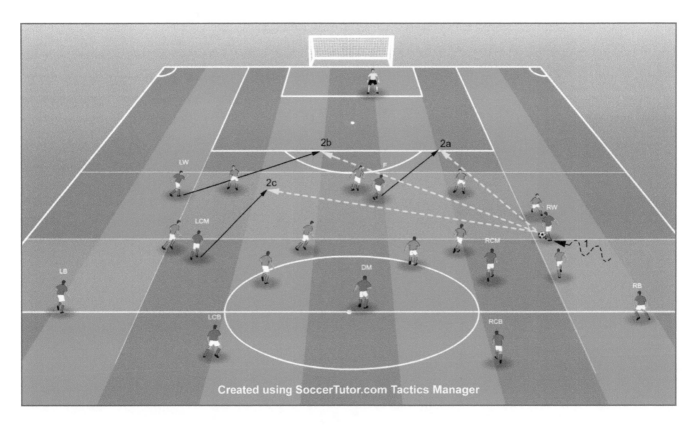

In the diagram above, we see the winger (RW) carrying the ball and moving toward the centre of the pitch. He has the following options to play a through pass in behind for a teammate:

A. **FORWARD:** Pass in behind and in between the opposition's full back and centre back for the diagonal run of the forward. The forward can receive in behind and take the ball into the penalty area for a 1 v 1 against the goalkeeper.

B. **OPPOSITE WINGER:** Pass in between the opposition's centre backs for the inside run of the opposite winger. The winger can also take the ball into the penalty area for a 1 v 1 against the goalkeeper

C. **CENTRAL MIDFIELDER:** A third option (not a pass in behind) is if the other 2 options are blocked. The pass to the left central midfielder (LCM) in space can either lead to a long distance shot or provide the opportunity for the LCM to then play a final pass in behind.

THE WINGER'S COMBINATION PLAY IN THE FINAL THIRD TO RECEIVE OR PLAY IN BEHIND

We now display the different combinations for the winger to consider if he is unable to simply play a through ball to a teammate, as shown on the previous page.

The winger in possession of the ball can consider the following tactical solutions:

1. Play a 1-2 combination to receive in behind

2. Combination play with 2 teammates + receiving in behind yourself

3. Play a 1-2 combination with closest teammate + pass in behind to that player

4. Play a 1-2 combination with closest teammate + pass in behind to a third player

The diagrams to follow display these different attacking solutions:

The opposing Left Back doesn't press the RW, so he is able to pass forward and receive in behind after a quick 1-2 with the Forward (F)

Created using SoccerTutor.com Tactics Manager

1-2 with Forward to Receive in Behind:

This is the easiest and best solution when there is little to no pressure on the ball from the opposing full back. If the red left back was closer to the ball, the pass to the forward would most likely be blocked off.

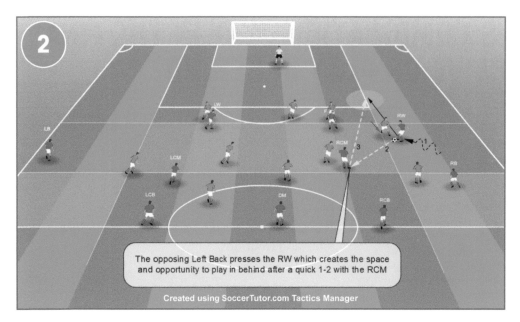

The opposing Left Back presses the RW which creates the space and opportunity to play in behind after a quick 1-2 with the RCM

Created using SoccerTutor.com Tactics Manager

1-2 with CM to Receive in Behind:

This time the opposing left back closes down our RW, so the pass to the forward is blocked off.

It also creates space behind the red left back to exploit.

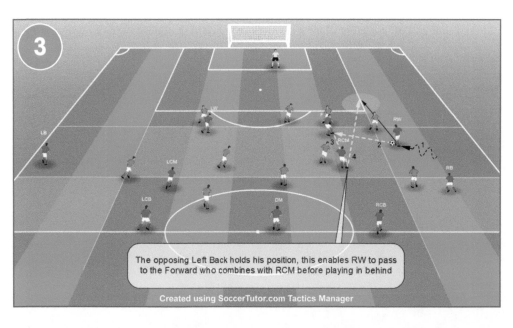

The opposing Left Back holds his position, this enables RW to pass to the Forward who combines with RCM before playing in behind

Created using SoccerTutor.com Tactics Manager

Pass, Lay-Off + Third Man Run to Receive in Behind:

This is a variation of example 1, as there is no pressure on the ball from the opposing full back.

This time, there is an extra pass before the RW receives in behind.

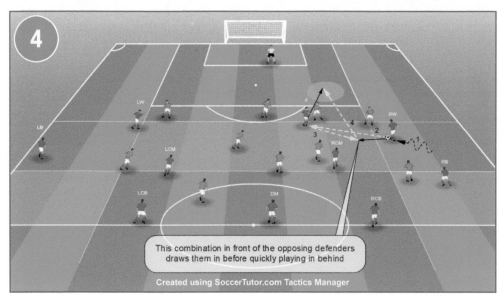

This combination in front of the opposing defenders draws them in before quickly playing in behind

Created using SoccerTutor.com Tactics Manager

1-2 with Forward + Pass in Behind:

This combination requires quick play with 1 touch passing - draw the opponents in and then quickly play in behind before they can react and reorganise.

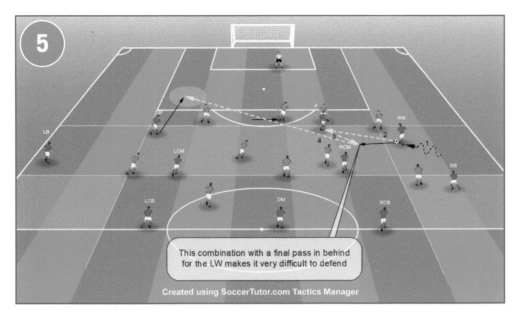

This combination with a final pass in behind for the LW makes it very difficult to defend

Created using SoccerTutor.com Tactics Manager

1-2 + Pass in Behind to Opposite Winger:

The original combination draws red defenders in with the right centre back shifting across.

This creates a gap between the red centre back and full back for our RW to pass in behind for the opposite winger (LW).

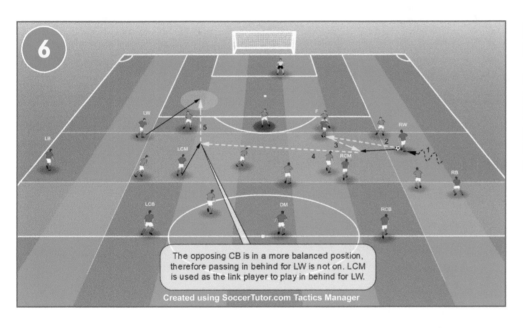

The opposing CB is in a more balanced position, therefore passing in behind for LW is not on. LCM is used as the link player to play in behind for LW.

Created using SoccerTutor.com Tactics Manager

1-2 + Pass Inside for CM:

In this variation of the previous example, there is no gap for the RW to play directly in behind to the LW, so the LCM is used as a "link player."

RW moving inside is ideal for creating the space for an overlapping run in behind

Created using SoccerTutor.com Tactics Manager

1-2 + Pass in Behind for the Overlapping Full Back:

By using advanced full backs in the 4-3-3 formation, you can create and exploit a numerical advantage high up on the flank.

In this variation, the RW still moves across to draw defenders inside to maximise the space on the flank

Created using SoccerTutor.com Tactics Manager

Pass, Lay-Off + Pass in Behind for the Overlapping Full Back:

This is a variation of the previous example, with the RCM playing the final pass this time.

1.4 - ATTACKING OPTIONS WHEN THE WINGER MOVES INSIDE TO RECEIVE BETWEEN THE LINES

The most common function of the winger is to receive a pass close to the sideline and then dribble the ball towards the opposing goal and develop playing combinations, as shown on the last few pages.

However, the winger can also move towards the middle (when positioned beyond the midfield line and/or in the attacking third), to get away from his direct opponent, and receive a direct entry pass ("imbucata"). The tactical solutions available to the winger are similar those we have already shown, with some differences:

1. Direct assist (through pass) for a teammate's run in behind

2. Play a 1-2 combination to receive in behind (and in the box)

3. Play a 1-2 combination + shoot from outside the penalty area

4. Play 1-2 combination with closest teammate + pass in behind to that player

5. Play a 1-2 combination with closest teammate + pass in behind for a third player

6. Combination play with 2 teammates to receive in behind

The diagrams to follow display these different attacking solutions.

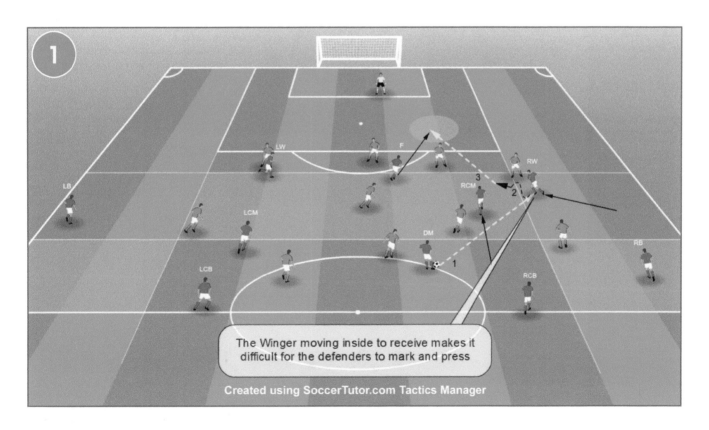

The Winger moving inside to receive makes it difficult for the defenders to mark and press

Created using SoccerTutor.com Tactics Manager

Through Pass in Behind for Forward:

As the winger (RW) takes the ball on the move, he is able to eliminate his direct opponent and play a final pass for the forward in the box.

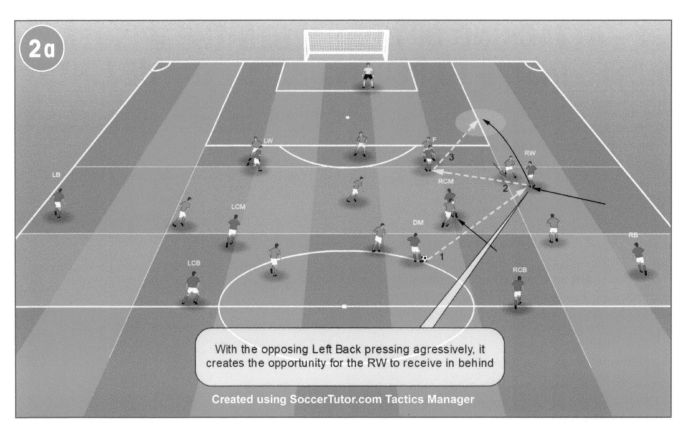

With the opposing Left Back pressing agressively, it creates the opportunity for the RW to receive in behind

Created using SoccerTutor.com Tactics Manager

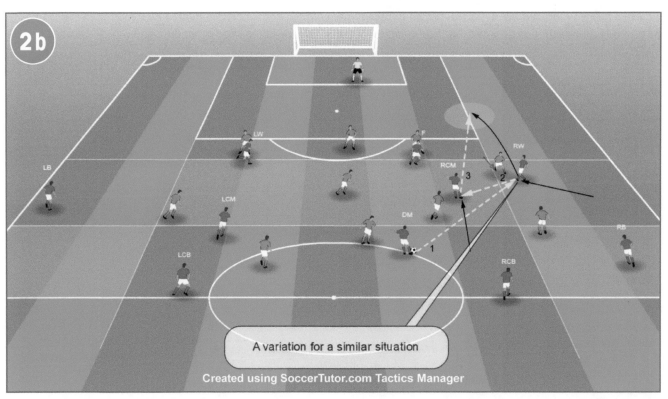

A variation for a similar situation

Created using SoccerTutor.com Tactics Manager

1-2 Combination to Receive in Behind:

In both situations, the opposing left back moves forward and out of position to contest our RW.

Therefore, the easiest and best option to get in behind is to play a quick 1-2, either with the forward (2a) or the RCM (2b).

In this situation, the nearest defenders press RW, therefore a quick shot at goal can be a good option to catch the GK off guard

Created using SoccerTutor.com Tactics Manager

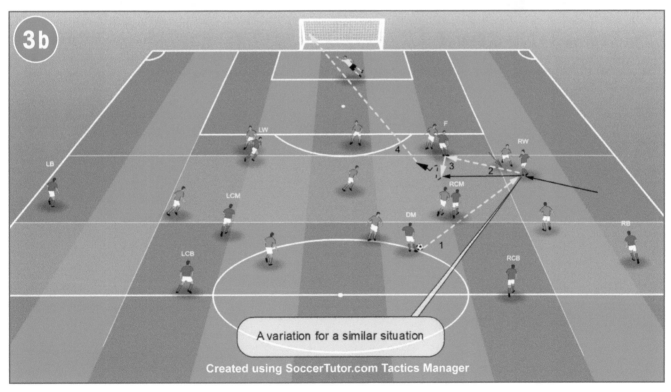

A variation for a similar situation

Created using SoccerTutor.com Tactics Manager

1-2 Combination + Shoot from Outside Box:

In both situations, the opposing defenders press aggressively, so the winger (RW) plays a quick 1-2, followed by a shot from outside the box.

3a and 3b show variations of the 1-2 combinations with the RCM and forward respectively.

Forward's movement to drop back a little and then quickly spin in behind for the return pass makes it difficult for the defenders to track

Created using SoccerTutor.com Tactics Manager

1-2 with Forward + Pass in Behind:

The winger (RW) moving inside and playing a quick 1-2 completely takes his direct opponent (red left back) out of the game.

After the 1-2, the RW is able to play a first time pass in behind for the forward, who has cleverly dropped back and then spun in behind to evade his marker.

Weight of pass and timing of runs are crucial for this goalscoring opportunity

Created using SoccerTutor.com Tactics Manager

In this variation, the RW plays a 1-2 with the forward instead and passes in behind (into box) for the opposite winger to finish

Created using SoccerTutor.com Tactics Manager

1-2 with Closest Teammate + Pass in Behind for a Third Player:

The winger's first pass should be to the correct foot of his teammate, so they can then play the next pass first time. Also, the next pass from the teammate must be out in front of the RW, so he can then play the final pass first time on the move.

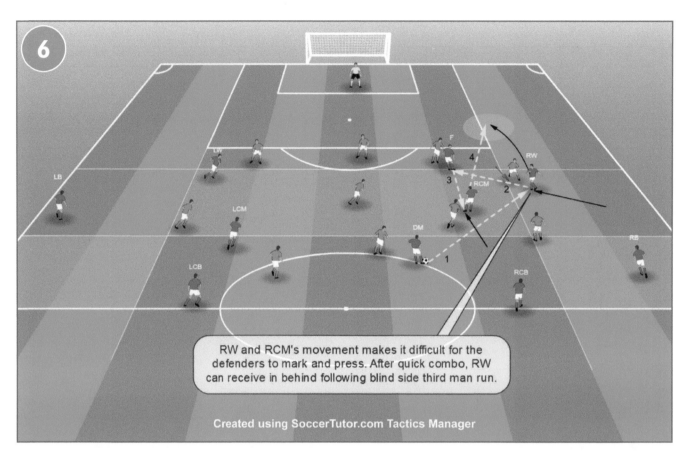

> RW and RCM's movement makes it difficult for the defenders to mark and press. After quick combo, RW can receive in behind following blind side third man run.

Created using SoccerTutor.com Tactics Manager

Combination Play with 2 Teammates to Receive in Behind with Third Man Run:

The RW is able to exploit the aggressive pressing of the opposing left back here by playing first time and then spinning in behind, making it very difficult to track him.

The RW's run in behind must be timed well to stay onside and receive the RCM's pass on the move.

1.5 - ATTACKING OPTIONS WHEN THE FORWARD RECEIVES AN "IMBUCATA" (VERTICAL) PASS

The "Imbucata" (entry ball) to the centre forward is a very effective way of accelerating an attacking move and for creating goal scoring opportunities.

The forward who receives the pass facing towards the goal or side-on to the opposition's defensive line has the following options:

1. Function as a rebounder and deflect the ball with a pass (or header) for a teammate, who makes a run in behind - <u>see diagram example below</u>.

2. Lay-off (pass ball back) for a teammate:

   • Play 1-2 and move to receive back in behind.

   • Lay-off the ball for the nearest player, who can then pass in behind for a third player.

   • Lay-off to a teammate to shoot from outside the penalty area.

In the following diagrams, we show the attacking options after an "Imbucata" pass to the forward.

The pass is timed well and the forward must be side on to "rebound" the ball into the path of the oncoming RW

Created using SoccerTutor.com Tactics Manager

First Time "Rebound Pass" in Behind for the Winger:

The open body shape of the forward is key, so he can see the pass coming, see the run of the RW and angle the pass in behind.

After an "Imbucata" pass, the forward needs fast support, so he can then play a first time pass to try and create goal scoring opportunities, and also limit the chances of his team losing possession.

I-2 with Winger to Receive in the Box:

The opposing left back marks our winger tightly when he moves inside, which creates space for the pass in behind.

RW and forward's movements are hard for the defenders to track - fast play to receive in behind

Created using SoccerTutor.com Tactics Manager

I-2 with CM to Receive in the Box:

When a central midfielder moves forward unmarked, this provides an easier option for the forward's lay-off, as there is more space available.

This is a varitation of the previous, with the forward now playing 1-2 with LCM

Created using SoccerTutor.com Tactics Manager

This shows how a forward's lay-off can be used to play in behind to another forward runner (LCM)

Created using SoccerTutor.com Tactics Manager

Lay-Off to Winger Who Crosses for CM's Run into the Box:

With this combination, the opposing defenders (RCB in particular) are dragged across, which creates space for the pass to our LCM.

This is a variation of the previous, with the lay-off to LCM and final ball to LW

Created using SoccerTutor.com Tactics Manager

Lay-Off to CM Who Can Shoot or Play a Through Pass to the Winger in the Box:

The opposing RCB is in a more balanced position here. Our LCM receives the lay-off and then plays in behind for a teammate (LW).

KEY POINTS:

After having highlighted some patterns of play aimed at completing the attacking move, it is appropriate to remember that the attacking phase must be a flexible process, with the coach and players ready to adjust to the different tactical situations that occur during the game.

We must remember the 3 different ways to finish an attack:

1. **WIDE ATTACK (CROSSING)**

2. **THROUGH BALL**

3. **SHOT FROM OUTSIDE THE PENALTY AREA**

When these conditions are in place, the players can choose the best and most appropriate option for the specific tactical situation at that point in the game.

When the execution of a move to finish an attack is not possible, the players must switch their focus to maintaining possession using a backward pass. From that point, still in possession, they can start a new attack - see the next section:

"2. OPTIONS BLOCKED: MAINTAIN POSSESSION AND START NEW ATTACK"

2. OPTIONS BLOCKED: MAINTAIN POSSESSION AND START NEW ATTACK

2. OPTIONS BLOCKED: MAINTAIN POSSESSION AND START NEW ATTACK

If it's not possible to break through the opposition's defensive line and the opposing players have stopped our efforts for a wide attack, an attack through the centre or to shoot from outside the penalty area, it is very important to provide continuity by maintaining possession of the ball and preparing the conditions to start a new attack.

We need to play the ball back to achieve this. It is necessary to build passing lanes:

- The player in possession must have a support player behind him who he can play the ball back to.

- There must also be another player available to receive from the ball carrier, in case the path to the first support player is blocked or he is tightly marked.

We classify the 2 back passes as follows:

1. **BACK PASS TO NEAREST SUPPORT PLAYER:**
Passing the ball back to the nearest support player allows the possibility of quickly attempting another attack. Alternatively, the team can simply focus on maintaining possession of the ball by passing to another close teammate.

2. **BACK PASS TO FURTHEST SUPPORT PLAYER:**
The team have to focus on simply maintaining possession of the ball and are at the starting point of a new attack.

The following diagrams show how to maintain possession, depending on the different tactical situations.

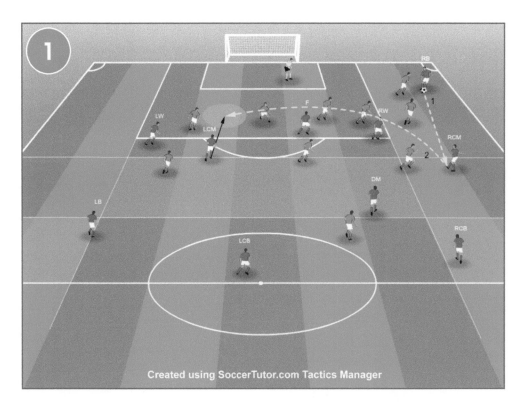

Created using SoccerTutor.com Tactics Manager

Pass to Nearest Support Player + Start Quick New Attack:

The player in possession (RB) passes back to the nearest support player (RCM). There is an opportunity to attack right away here, with the central midfielder's (RCM) cross into the box.

This option is recommended when the opposition's defensive line moves up after the pass back to a support player (RB's pass to RCM). This creates space for the LCM to run into and score from the cross.

Pass to Nearest Support Player + 1-2 to Shoot at Goal:

RCM receives and plays a 1-2 with RW and receives back towards the centre. This gives him the opportunity to shoot from outside the box.

This option is particularly useful when the opposition's defence do not move up after the back pass to the support player (RB's pass to RCM).

Pass to Nearest Support Player + Pass to Furthest Support Player:

The third option for RCM is to simply play the ball all the way back to the centre back (RCB).

This allows for the team to maintain possession when there are no options to quickly start a new attack.

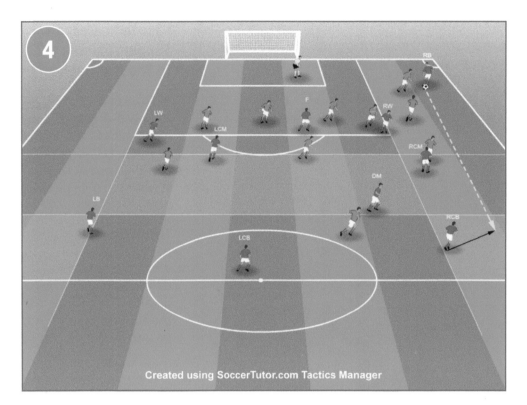

Pass to Furthest Support Player to Reset Attack:

The nearest support player (RCM) is marked tightly. With the objective of restarting the move, it's important to maintain possession, as mentioned earlier. Therefore, we want to use passes with limited risks.

So, in this example, we see the player in possession of the ball (RB) passing directly back to the centre back (RCB).

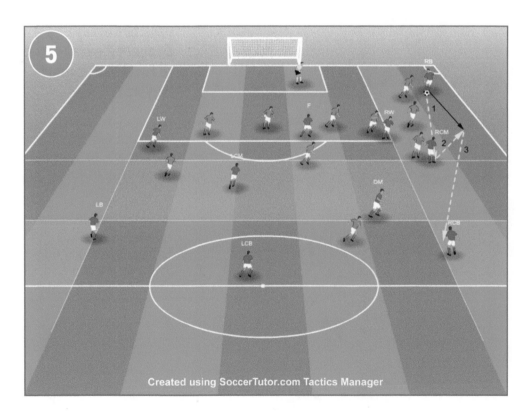

I-2 Combination with Nearest Support Player + Pass Back to Reset:

We conclude the options for playing the ball back with combination play that makes it possible to move the ball from the attacking third back into the middle third of the pitch.

In this situation, the player in possession (RB) passes the ball to the nearest support player (RCM), receives it back and then passes back to the centre back (RCB) to reset and restart a new attack.

3. FINISHING

3. FINISHING

TRANSFORMING AN OPEN BALL SITUATION INTO A SHOT ON GOAL

The following options are available when the player in possession has available space and time in an open ball situation:

1. The player without the ball moves in behind or in between the lines to receive a final pass (assist).

2. The player in possession plays the final pass.

However, this opportunity is not always possible, in that the opponent could react by blocking the passing lane.

If the passing lane is blocked, the players must read the tactical situation and use alternate choices:

1. The player without the ball moves towards the ball to receive a pass to feet.

2. The player in possession plays the ball to the feet of the receiver, and moves to another position to create space, or receive a pass back.

At the moment the receiver gets the ball, he can fundamentally make 3 choices:

1. Control the ball and shoot at goal.

2. Return the ball to his teammate.

3. Pass the ball to a third teammate.

It is appropriate to use the first option when the direct opponent provides this opportunity and when there are good possibilities for a dangerous shot at goal.

If, instead, it's not possible to shoot, the priority is to pass to a teammate. This can be accomplished with a direct pass or with the participation of a third teammate. The best choice depends on the timing and movements of the players.

Initially, after passing to a teammate, the player in possession can:

1. Make a run in behind the defensive line to receive the return pass.

2. Move in between the lines, in order to receive in a favourable position in front of the opposition's defensive line.

Even in this situation, the choice between the 2 options depends on the reaction (real and potential) of the direct opponent:

1. If the direct opponent can be attacked behind his back, the player must make a run in behind, hoping to receive the return pass from the teammate he passed to, or from a third teammate who has joined the combination.

2. If, instead, the opponent cannot be attacked in behind, the most appropriate choice for the player in possession relates to repositioning in between the lines and making himself available to receive the return pass in the space in front of the defensive line.

When a player does receive in front of the opposition's defensive line in an open ball situation, he has the following options:

1. Shoot from outside the penalty area.

2. Provide an assist for the teammate that passed him the ball.

3. Provide an assist for a third teammate.

FINISHING: THE DECISIVE MOMENT

Finishing is the decisive moment of a move which may have required time, energy and the correct decision making for its development.

To be more effective than the opponent on the pitch in carrying out various processes, but not effective enough in the finishing process, is a problem that can have a determining impact on the result of a match.

For these reasons, I always remind coaches that finishing may not the most important aspect of the attacking phase, but it has an enormous impact on the final score.

The finishing of an action requires the player in possession to be focused on the objective and select (at the moment of the shot) the right trajectory, combining power and precision, in order to beat the opposing goalkeeper.

The finishing of an action, from a technical-tactical standpoint, requires various skills that must allow the player to finish in a positive way.

The player must be able to finish:

- With both feet or head

- From long, medium and short distances

- After dribbling the ball

- After controlling/receiving with 1 touch

- "First time"

- With the goalkeeper on the goal line or coming off the line

- Under close pressure or without pressure

EXAMPLE: After Dribbling the Ball with GK Coming Off His Line

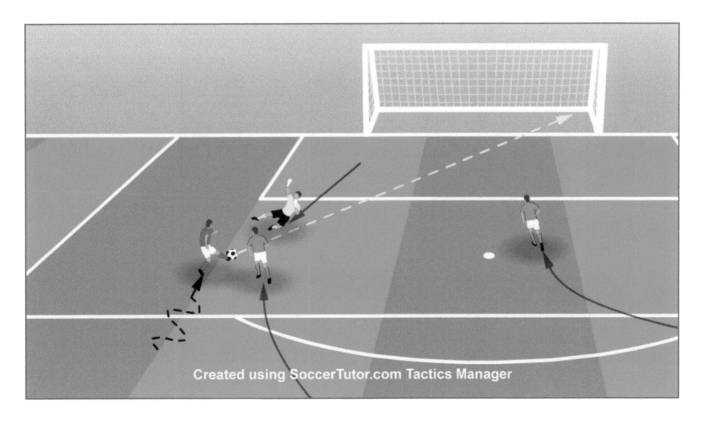

Created using SoccerTutor.com Tactics Manager

CROSSING THE BALL INTO THE PENALTY AREA AND FINISHING

The 4-3-3 formation only has 1 centre forward and it is important that this player be well supported by lateral passes (crosses) from his teammates.

In particular, it is of fundamental importance to have the forward attack the front post for 2 basic reasons:

1. It is the ideal position for finishing on goal, with the feet or head.

2. Positioning a player in this zone (as we shall see in the analysis of the defensive phase) keeps 2 opposing defenders occupied.

With the centre forward attacking the front post, it is very important to have the winger on the opposite side attacking the far post and the central midfielder from the opposite side move near the penalty spot (another favourable zone for finishing a cross).

The player that crosses the ball (whether it is the full back, the winger or a central midfielder) must have a supporting player behind him, while the centre back is always available to return the ball all the way back to a reset and start a new attack.

The winger or central midfielder on this side (the strong side), who is not delivering the cross, takes up a useful position at the edge of the penalty area to receive any clearances or rebounds.

In addition, all players behind the line of the ball need to take up intelligent positions and use preventative marking in case possession is lost and the opposition are able to launch a counter attack.

Attacking Runs and Positioning from a Wide Cross

Created using SoccerTutor.com Tactics Manager

- **Right Back (RB):** Delivers Cross

- **Right Central Mid. (RCM):** Support

- **Right Winger (RW):** Positioned outside the box for rebounds

- **Forward (F):** Front Post

- **Left Winger (LW):** Back Post

- **Left Central Mid. (LCM):** Penalty Spot

PRACTICE EXAMPLES FOR THE FINISHING PHASE

I. Attacking Combination in a Position Specific Passing Drill

Created using SoccerTutor.com Tactics Manager

Objective: Passing, pattern play, combination play with lay-offs, crossing and finishing.

Practice Description

We divide half a pitch vertically and have 5 or 6 players on each side. The players take up their approximate positions on the pitch and the 2 groups use different passing combinations simultaneously, ending with a finish or shot at goal.

The diagram shows 2 possible combinations with the 4-3-3 formation:

- **LEFT (Combination Play with Lay-offs + Shot from Outside Penalty Area):**

The centre back (LCB) plays an aerial pass to the winger (LW), who lays the ball off to the forward running left back (LB). The left back passes to the forward (F), who lays the ball off to the central midfielder (LCM) and he shoots from outside the penalty area.

- **RIGHT (Working the Ball Wide for Cross + Finish):**

The centre back (RCB) plays a short pass to the defensive midfielder (DM). The DM passes to the winger (RW) who has moved inside. The RW lays the ball off to the central midfielder (RCM), who plays a forward pass to the right back (RB). The RB makes an overlapping run high up the flank. To complete the sequence, the RB crosses for the forward (F) to finish.

* You can use various different combinations - please see tactical examples in this chapter as a good reference.

2. Possession Play + Fast Attack in Behind the Opposition's Defence in a Dynamic Practice

After 6-8 passes, look to get in behind and finish

Created using SoccerTutor.com Tactics Manager

Objective: Possession play, timing passes/runs in behind the defence and finishing.

Practice Description

Using half a full pitch, we mark out a large zone (1) the width of the penalty area and a small zone (2) which is the full width of the pitch.

In zone 1, we have a 4 v 4 situation +2 yellow neutral players who play with the team in possession and act as the centre back and forward.

There are also 2 yellow neutral wingers (LW & RW) outside the zone in the positions shown and 3 opposing red defenders in front of the penalty area (inside zone 2).

The practice starts with the coach's pass. The blue attacking team have to:

- Complete 8-10 passes within zone 1 with help from the neutral players. If the red defending team win the ball, the practice continues with the team roles reversed.

- Pass the ball to one of the neutral wingers who have to make a run in behind the 3 opposing defenders to receive (RW in diagram example). The 3 red defenders can intercept the ball, but they are not allowed to leave their zone. The aim is to finish the attack as quickly as possible, with players making runs to support.

3. Crossing and Finishing in a 5 v 5 (+2) Positional Small Sided Game with Side Zones

Created using SoccerTutor.com Tactics Manager

Objective: Exploiting width in attack, crossing and finishing.

Practice Description

Using the area shown, we mark out 2 side zones where we have yellow neutral players (full backs - FB).

In the main middle zone, we have a 5 v 5 situation (+2 GKs in large goals). The goalkeepers act as the defensive midfielder (DM), we have 2 central midfielders (LCM/RCM), 2 wingers (LW/RW) and 1 forward (F).

The wide neutral players act as full backs (LB/RB) and only play with the team in possession.
* There are no centre backs for this practice.

1. The practice starts from the coach or the goalkeeper.

2. The team in possession (blues in diagram) aim to score a goal with help from the neutral players (7 v 5 advantage).

3. The practice emphasis is on using the numerical advantage and getting the ball wide to the neutral players quickly. From there, the neutral players deliver crosses and for the players to try and finish. There should be continuous crosses in this game.

4. If the defending team wins the ball at any time, the team roles are reversed and the practice continues.

4. Continuous Shooting and Finishing in a 3 Team "Winner Stays On" Game

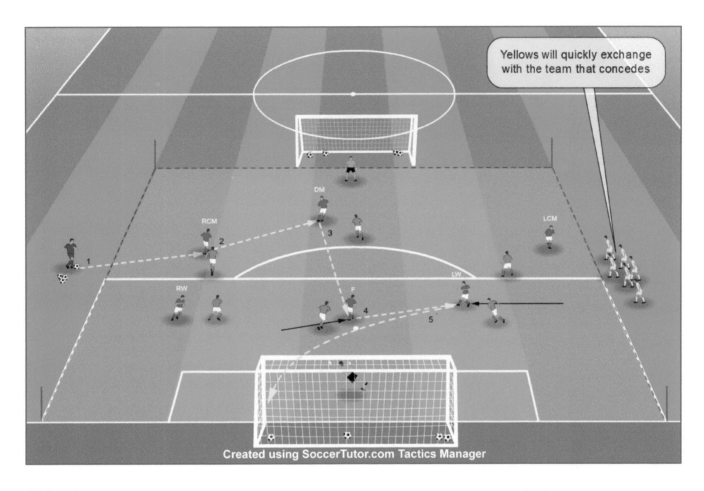

Yellows will quickly exchange with the team that concedes

Created using SoccerTutor.com Tactics Manager

Objective: Improve finishing in the box (in similar situations to competitive matches).

Practice Description

In an area double the size of the penalty box, we have 2 teams (blues vs reds) competing against each other. Outside of the area, there is a third team of 6 yellow players.

The teams play a high tempo game with the emphasis on shooting quickly, as soon as there is space available.

This game is "First Goal Wins" and "Winner Stays On."

The team that concedes a goal (reds in diagram example) will have to leave the area and switch with the third team (yellows) that is waiting outside.

The yellows will then play the blues and the team that concedes will leave the pitch. The game carries on like this.

5. Maintain Possession and Start a New Attack When Options Are Blocked in a Dynamic Practice

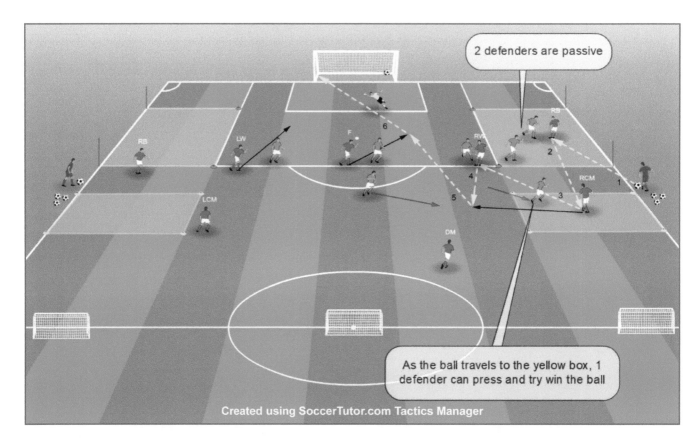

Objective: Adapting to the tactical situation when attacking options are blocked, providing support, maintaining possession, resetting attacks and starting new attacks.

Practice Description

The blue attacking team have all their players from the 4-3-3 formation, except the goalkeeper and centre backs. The red defending team have a goalkeeper and 7 outfield players - you can adapt their formation to that of your next opponents.

1. The practice starts with the coach's pass into one of the white boxes. In there, we have 1 blue full back (RB in diagram example) and 2 red players who simply apply passive pressure.

2. The RB has 2 options:
   a. Pass into the yellow box for the central midfielder (RCM).
   b. Pass all the way back to the DM.

3. Once the RCM receives inside the yellow box, 1 red player is allowed to move into the box to press. The blue RCM will then make the best decision:
   a. Start a new attack, as shown in the diagram example: 1-2 with RW and final pass in behind for forward.
   b. Pass back to the DM to reset.
   c. <u>**More options are displayed on pages 136-138**</u>.

4. The practice then restarts on the left side with the same objectives.

CHAPTER 6

THE DEFENSIVE PHASE

THE DEFENSIVE PHASE: PRELIMINARY CONSIDERATIONS

Before proceeding with the analysis, it's necessary to make some preliminary considerations.

The attacking phase and defensive phase are not 2 completely separate tactical situations. Actually, the interpretation of attacking movements influences defensive approaches significantly, and vice versa.

A team capable of staying compact thanks to the ability to maintain possession of the ball with adequate ball circulation will be more ready, mentally and physically. They will be able to press their opponents with determination as soon as they lose possession of the ball.

This is in contrast to a team, for example, that prefers to play mostly with long balls, as this would cause the distance between their defensive, midfield and attacking sectors to be large and negatively affect their transition from attack to defence.

Another factor to keep in mind is the fact that the team in possession of the ball can control the game and dictate the "tempo" of the game.

The effectiveness of contrasting that situation depends on the choices made by the defending team and the level/ability of the players. Against opponents that are not particularly advanced, it may be possible to recover the ball quite easily.

This and other considerations must be kept in mind when determining the strategy of the game. Some coaches prefer leaving the control of the ball to the opposing team, so they are ready to exploit spaces created by the team in possession, while they move the ball around.

Other coaches like to dominate their opponents and dictate the rhythm of the game throughout, even though they know the that this will most likely limit the space behind the opposition's defence and actually open up the risk of being vulnerable to counter attacks.

DEFENSIVE PROCESSES

For the defensive processes, there are 2 tactical situations to consider:

1. POSITIONAL DEFENDING

Positional defending takes place when the team has all or almost all of their players behind the line of the ball. This happens when our team has sufficient time to reposition themselves after losing possession.

Below is a list of situations when the team will generally be able to reposition all the players behind the line of the ball:

- Attack ended with the ball going out for a goal kick for the opposition.

- Attack ended with the ball going out for a throw-in for the opposition.

- Commit a foul resulting in a free kick for the opposition.

- After playing a long pass into the opposition's half with most players in defensive organisation.

- The opponents choose to build a positional attack (not a counter attack).

2. DEFENSIVE REORGANISATION

Defensive reorganisation takes place when we lose possession in open play and our team is only partially behind the line of the ball. In this situation, it is necessary for our players to reorganise instead of use positional defending.

In this situation, fundamentally there are 2 choices:

- **Withdraw** (get back behind ball and into shape)

The withdrawal takes place when the opponent has the potential to launch a counter attack. The players behind the ball withdraw (move back collectively) to reduce the space available in behind and delay the opposition's counter attack.

This also gives time for their teammates who are ahead of the line of the ball to get back and help defend, restoring defensive balance to try and recover the ball.

- **Aggressive Reaction** (reactive pressing)

The aggressive reaction can be used when we have many players around the ball zone at the point possession is lost.

We use aggressive pressing in numbers when it's possible to put immediate pressure on the opposing player in possession of the ball and also close the passing lanes to his nearby support players.

When using aggressive pressing, the opposition will most likely then look to play long passes to teammates higher up the pitch and ahead of the line of the ball.

It is therefore key for our defenders to use aggressive marking on their attacking players also, condensing the space and hopefully recovering the ball as quickly as possible. The whole team must be aware and use the same tactics to have continuity and for the aggressive pressing to be successful.

PRESSING

COUNTERACTING OPPONENT'S MOVEMENTS IN VARIOUS ZONES AND PRESSING TYPES

Generally, pressing is organised into the zones in which it occurs, in relation to the part of the pitch where this defensive action takes place.

- If the defending team presses their opponents in the high zone close to the penalty area, it is called **"Ultra-Offensive Pressing"**

- If the pressing takes place in the middle zone, it is called **"Offensive Pressing"**

- If the pressing takes place in the low zone and close to our goal, it is called **"Defensive Pressing"**

We are going to analyse 3 processes (pressing, compactness and winning the ball) and, to make their understanding clearer, we shall associate them with the following 3 zones:

- **HIGH ZONE** (attacking third of the pitch)

- **MIDDLE ZONE** (middle third of the pitch)

- **LOW ZONE** (defensive third of the pitch)

Regarding the different styles of pressing, we identify these 3 types:

1. REACTIVE PRESSING

Reactive pressing relates to the team's reaction at the moment it loses possession of the ball (transition from attack to defence).

2. ADVANCED PRESSING

Advanced pressing relates to positional defending and countering the opponent's actions that have started in their half of the pitch.

3. DEFENSIVE PRESSING

Defensive pressing relates to positional defending and identifies the defensive action in our half of the pitch.

COUNTERACTING PHASE

Before the ball is put back in play i.e. Goal kick, the team must understand where the opposing players are positioned and whether they are able to isolate our defensive unit. This depends on the strategic positioning of the opposing forwards.

If this happens, we have to decide whether to accept the numerical equality we have at the back and encourage the opposing team to a play a long ball.

If we want to have a numerical advantage at the back, we have to take precautions, in order to counter this situation, following a short distribution from the opposition's goalkeeper. This relates to players moving into different positions and changing the team shape/formation to counter our opponents.

Along these lines, it is necessary to decide on the best deployment (positioning) of our players to lead the opponent to:

- Play the ball towards the zone of the pitch more favourable to us (the next step is to use advanced pressing which is fully explained on the next page).

- Or pass towards a player with a low skill level.

CLOSING DOWN PHASE

The "Closing Down Phase" is clearly related to the opponent's system of play (formation) and their positioning for a restart if they won the ball from us as a result of the ball being kicked out of play, rather than being recovered in open play during the development of our possession/attacking phase.

In the next section, we display our pressing solutions to shorten the marking distances to our opponents, according to their system of play (4-4-2, 4-3-3, 4-3-1-2, 4-2-3-1 and 3-5-2).

ADVANCED PRESSING HIGH UP THE PITCH

Against teams that can move the ball with precision at a fast pace (and let's remember that the ball "does not get tired" and can run "faster" than any player), know how to utilise their goalkeeper as a withdrawn playmaker and often manage to move the ball to players in between the lines…it is useless, and dangerous, to use advanced and aggressive pressing in their half of the pitch.

However, pressing in the opposition's half can be done successfully against teams with limited technical and tactical ability.

In these situations, it is important to adopt a defensive approach that enables us to:

- Advanced pressing of the ball carrier.

- Cover the space of the nearest opponent who is left unmarked.

- Close down any players that can function as support players.

- Block/limit passing lanes through tight marking.

- Create a numerical advantage around the ball zone by shifting players across from the weak side.

- Neutralise potential long balls (opponent's direct or accelerated build up) through appropriate marking of the opposing forwards. This should not be done by defenders via advanced marking, as they need to also be aware to defend the space in behind them.

PRESSING WITH THE 4-3-3 AGAINST DIFFERENT FORMATIONS

I. PRESSING AGAINST THE 4-4-2

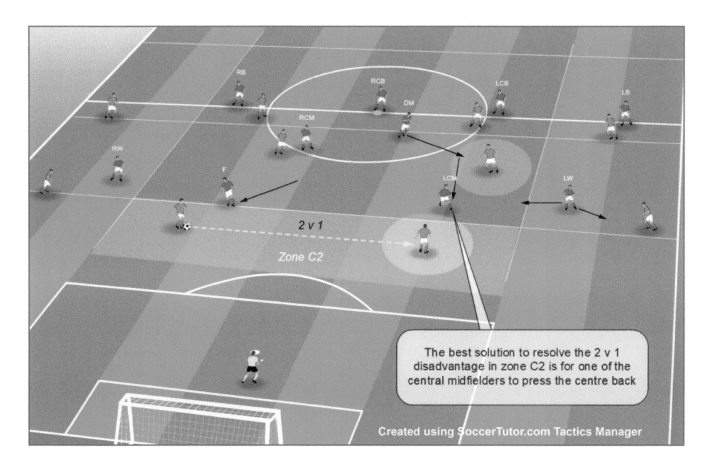

2 v 1

Zone C2

The best solution to resolve the 2 v 1 disadvantage in zone C2 is for one of the central midfielders to press the centre back

Created using SoccerTutor.com Tactics Manager

Against the 4-4-2 formation, the opposition have a 2 v 1 numerical advantage in Zone C2 with 2 centre backs against our 1 forward. One of the opposing centre backs is most likely to receive in space and dribble forward with the ball.

The best solution for this problem is to press the centre back in possession by having a central midfielder push forward to contest him (LCM in diagram example).

Obviously this movement has to be executed with the right timing, and we want to address the related details:

Firstly, it is important to know that, if the central midfielder in question (LCM) has to cover several yards/metres to get close to the opposing centre back with the ball, the opposing midfielder who is subsequently left unmarked could have plenty of time to move into another position, creating a passing lane for the centre back to easily pass the ball to him.

Therefore, it is recommended to move forward before the opposing player receives and also have a plan for our players' subsequent movements to press collectively and cover each other.

The whole sequence is shown in the diagram above. The forward (F) starts moving toward the centre back with the ball, inviting him to either send a long ball forward or pass to the other centre back.

If the opponents go for the second option and the ball is passed to the other centre back, our central midfielder (LCM) moves aggressively toward the receiver before he receives the ball.

Our central midfielder (LCM) will also try to "block" the passing lane toward the unmarked opposing midfielder at the same time. In addition, our defensive midfielder (DM) moves closer to the opposing midfielder to prevent him from receiving, while the winger (LW) can move towards the centre to provide additional cover.

2. PRESSING AGAINST THE 4-3-3

Block the passing lanes

Created using SoccerTutor.com Tactics Manager

In a similar situation to the previous one, but now against the 4-3-3 formation, not only do we have to put pressure on the ball carrier and block the passing lane towards the central midfielder, we also have to block the passing lane towards the opposing defensive midfielder.

To counteract this tactical situation, it is convenient to invert the orientation of the triangle shape in our midfield, with our defensive midfielder (DM) moving forward to mark his counterpart on the opposing team, as soon as the opponents start building from the back.

As in the previous situation, our central midfielder (LCM) moves forward to press the centre back before he receives the pass from his teammate.

With our central midfielder (LCM) moving forward to press the new ball carrier, the opposing central midfielder (RCM) is the likely target of the pass from the centre back. Our full back on that side (LB in

this situation) has to be ready to advance quickly towards the opposing midfielder, as soon as it becomes clear that he will receive the ball.

This adjustment by the LB is aggressive, but it is a necessary approach if we are determined to create problems for the opponents' build up play in their half of the pitch.

HOWEVER, if our other centre back (RCB) cannot handle matching up with the opposing centre forward (who could be very fast), it may be better to drop the defensive line, limiting the free space in behind our defence.

If their central midfielder (RCM) moves wider to receive a pass in the flank zone, our winger (LW) moves towards the centre to contest him and prevent him from receiving a pass.

3. PRESSING AGAINST THE 4-3-1-2

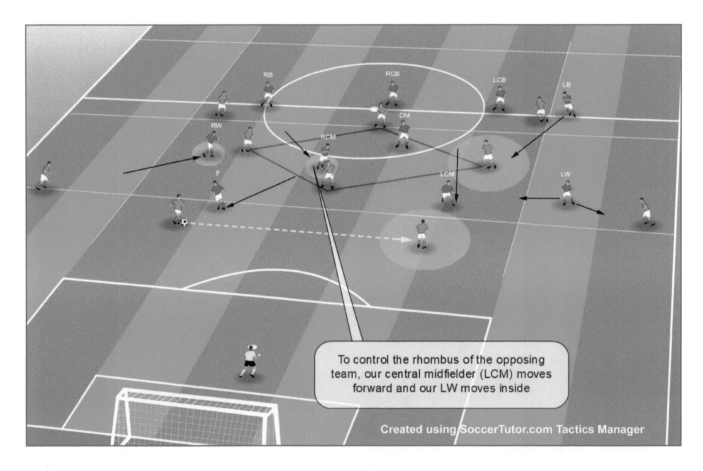

To control the rhombus of the opposing team, our central midfielder (LCM) moves forward and our LW moves inside

Created using SoccerTutor.com Tactics Manager

To play against a team using the 4-3-1-2 formation involves not only balancing numbers with respect to the opposing 2 centre backs, but also a good strategy to control the rhombus (diamond) of the opposing team in midfield.

As with the 2 previous situations, our central midfielder (LCM) moves forward to press the centre back before he receives the pass.

The difference here is that our other central midfielder (RCM) also moves forward to press the opposing defensive midfielder. This movement is compensated by the winger on that side (RW) moving inside, as shown.

Our defensive midfielder (DM) remains in his position, marking the opposing attacking midfielder, while also controlling the opposing right central midfielder.

The player that actually contests the opposing right central midfielder depends on his movements in relation to the positioning/movements of the forwards. If the forwards remain in a central position, our full back (LB) moves forward and towards the centre, ready to contest the opposing midfielder (as shown in the diagram).

HOWEVER, if instead one forward has moved quite wide, thus "occupying" our left back (LB), one of our 2 centre backs moves forward to control/contest the opposing right central midfielder or, alternatively, marks the attacking midfielder, with the defensive midfielder pushing forward to press the right central midfielder.

The winger on the strong side (LW) moves inside to create an obstacle for the right central midfielder, who may drop back and then open up toward the flank to receive.

4. PRESSING AGAINST THE 4-2-3-1

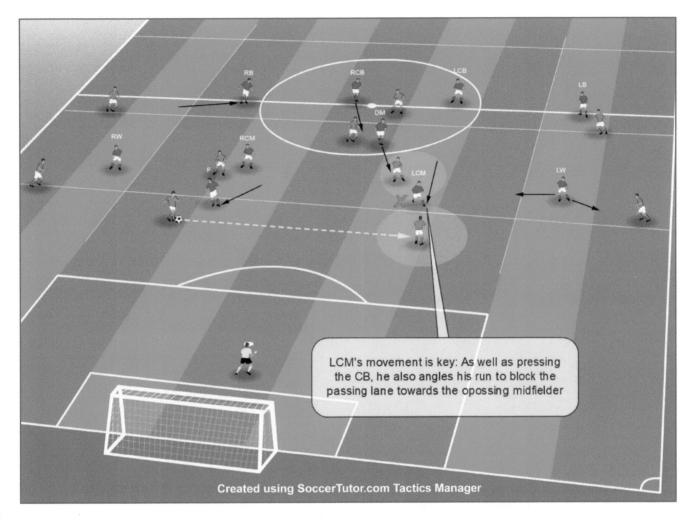

LCM's movement is key: As well as pressing the CB, he also angles his run to block the passing lane towards the opossing midfielder

Created using SoccerTutor.com Tactics Manager

Pressing against the 4-2-3-1 formation mostly follows the same principles seen for contesting the 4-4-2 formation (**see page 156**).

The major difference is the presence of 1 centre forward and a No.10 instead of 2 centre forwards.

Even in this situation, in the central area of the pitch, the most logical choice is still for the central midfielder (LCM in diagram example) to move forward to press the centre back before he receives the pass from his teammate.

Our central midfielder (LCM) will also try to "block" the passing lane toward the unmarked opposing midfielder at the same time. In addition, our defensive midfielder (DM) moves closer to the opposing midfielder to prevent him from receiving,

while the winger (LW) moves towards the middle to provide additional cover.

One of the centre backs (RCB in diagram example) moves forward and close to the red No.10 to compensate for our defensive midfielder's forward movement.

The other centre back (LCB) protects the space in behind and the full back on the weak side (RB) moves closer to the centre to provide balance in defence.

5. PRESSING AGAINST THE 3-5-2

LCM'S movement is key: As well as pressing the CB, he also angles his run to block the passing lane towards the opossing midfielder

Created using SoccerTutor.com Tactics Manager

When playing against the 3-5-2 formation, there is a potential numerical advantage for our opponents in their back line, with their defensive midfielder supporting the 3 centre backs.

The proposed solutions, as shown in the diagram, are as follows:

- Our wingers (RW & LW) control their wide centre backs.

- Our forward (F) covers the defensive midfielder.

- The opposing centre back with the ball is pressed by our central midfielder (LCM in diagram).

- Our defensive midfielder moves forward to mark the opposing right central midfielder.

- If the opposing right central midfielder opens up towards the flank, our full back (LB) will move towards the centre.

Thanks to the movement of our full back on the weak side (RB) towards the centre, our defensive unit has a numerical advantage over the opposing 2 forwards.

KEY POINT:

Naturally, all of the tactical solutions we have presented in this section look good on paper, but only after careful evaluation of the 2 teams on the pitch (our team and the opposing team), can you truly make it possible to prepare a fully accurate plan of action to organise all the different shifting of marking responsibilities.

DEFENSIVE
COMPACTNESS

COMPACTING PHASE: KEEPING SHORT DISTANCES BETWEEN PLAYERS AND LINES

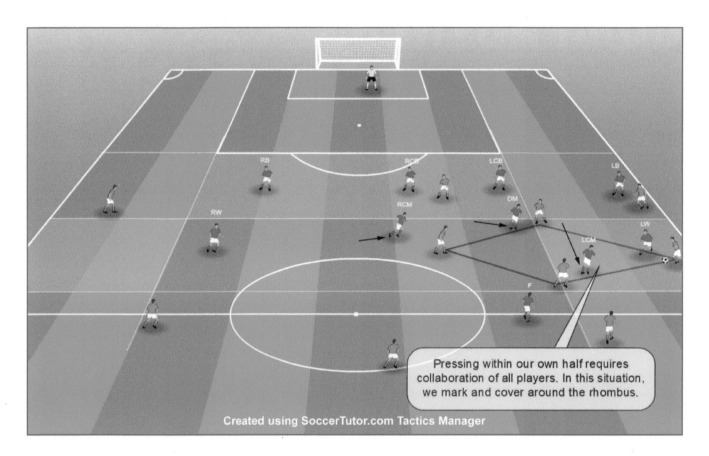

Pressing within our own half requires collaboration of all players. In this situation, we mark and cover around the rhombus.

Created using SoccerTutor.com Tactics Manager

An alternative to advanced pressing is to press in our half of the pitch. The advantage of this approach is mainly that the opponents have less space to attack behind our defence. Consequently, it becomes less probable to be subject to a direct attack. The process of defensive compactness includes 2 phases:

1. **Compacting Phase**

2. **Prevention Phase**

During the compacting phase, the top priority is to keep the different sectors of the team (defence, midfield, attack) close to each other. The team will be compact and there will be short distances between our players and lines. The opponents will try to direct the play between our midfield and defensive lines, which we focus on preventing.

In order to optimise the compacting phase, we must have the collaboration of all players. In particular, the wingers will have to be ready to come back, while the midfielders will have to "swing" forward

and backward, with the objective of blocking passing lanes for the opponents. Specifically, it is very important to keep the following in mind:

- Dynamism of defensive line, ready to adapt to the movement of the ball and ready to move forward.

- Keep the formation "compact" when the ball moves towards the opposing goal.

- Ability of our midfielders to "deactivate" the potential damage of the rhombus shapes that the opponents try to form. It is important to mark/cover the opposing players who occupy the front support and back support in these rhombus shapes.

- Our forward needs to alternate his role in pressing the back support of the rhombus and, at the same time, be ready to get free, for when he thinks that his teammates can recover the ball and launch a counter attack.

PREVENTION PHASE: LIMITING TIME AND SPACE AROUND THE BALL

When the opposing team play forward between the lines, our team need to react quickly, press the ball carrier and limit the time and space in and around the ball + block any attempt to pass in behind our defence.

Created using SoccerTutor.com Tactics Manager

Naturally, in addition to being compact to make it more difficult for the opponents to play between the lines, our team must be organised and be able to react to the opponent's attempt of increasing the pace of the game.

When this happens and the opposing team directs the play behind our midfield line, our players have to quickly block attempts to create conditions for an open ball situation and a final pass in behind.

To prevent this, it fundamentally means that we have to limit the time and space around the potential receivers in the rhombus shape and their closest teammates.

All this can be pursued through the following measures:

- The collective reaction of the defensive unit to limit time, space and options around the ball.

- Press the ball carrier.

- Block possible passing lanes in behind or that could help attacking combinations.

- Midfielders must react and move back, so that, in collaboration with the back line, they can compress the space available for the opposition players.

DEFENSIVE REACTIONS (COLLECTIVE AND INDIVIDUAL)

DEFENSIVE REACTIONS (COLLECTIVE AND INDIVIDUAL)

The moment when the opponent tries to finish their attack and convert an open ball situation into a shot on goal, it is of fundamental importance to energetically stop this attempt and intercept (win) the ball.

Winning the ball includes 2 phases:

1. **COLLECTIVE REACTIONS OF THE DEFENSIVE LINE:** This is basically correlated with the solutions and the reactions that the defensive line must produce against the developments of the opposing team.

2. **REACTIONS OF INDIVIDUAL DEFENDERS:** This phase relates more closely to the individual choices and the ability of defenders to contest their direct opponents.

I. COLLECTIVE REACTIONS OF THE DEFENSIVE LINE

Without going too deeply into specific details, here we show the common situations that the defensive line will face. The back line must know how to react, depending on the movements of the ball. When the ball moves horizontally from one side to the other, the back line must know how to move collectively.

A. **Ball is moved from the flank into the centre:** Defensive line returns to its normal starting shape and positioning

B. **Ball is moved from centre of pitch to the flank:** Line shifts collectively across, keeping close distances between each other

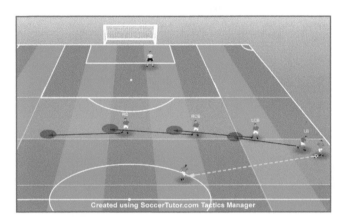

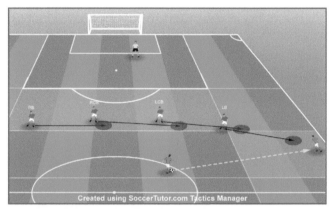

C. **Long Pass Back:** Defensive line moves collectively forward

D. **Short Pass Back:** Defensive line simply readjusts its position by a similar distance

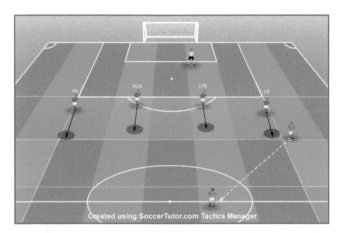

KEY POINT:

When the ball advances towards our defensive line, they must collectively reorganise, while evaluating these 3 fundamental parameters:

1. The freedom of play for the player in possession of the ball: Does he have an open ball situation or a closed ball situation?

2. The distance from the player in possession.

3. The actual position of the defensive line on the pitch and the space available to the opponent, in case they decide to attack in behind.

2. REACTIONS OF INDIVIDUAL DEFENDERS

In this phase, we work on decision making and the ability of defenders to anticipate and contest their direct opponents.

This is the last opportunity to stop the opponent's attempt to shoot at goal and the individual intervention has a special priority.

The player involved is the direct defender against the opposing individual who is about to shoot on goal, and of course his ability to be in the correct position and contest the opponent is fundamental.

These are the main 2 situations involving our defenders:

1. **The opponent is about to receive the ball and finish the attack.**

2. **The opponent is already in possession of the ball and is getting ready to shoot at goal.**

In the first situation, the defender must try to stop the opponent receiving the ball, whereas in the second situation he has to stop the shot at goal.

These are different game situations that the players must resolve, keeping in mind the various parameters that characterise these situations (distance from goal, characteristics of the opponent, position of teammates, etc.).

In the first situation, the objective for the defender is to anticipate the opponent's movement.

The defender of course would have to stay in contact with his teammates in the defensive line and understand when to "take off" to apply tight marking of the individual opponent.

In the 2 diagrams below, we show situations where a centre back behaves in 2 different ways.

A. Man Marking: Centre Back moves forward to contest direct opponent

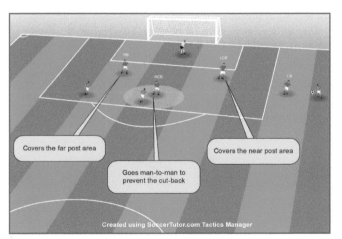

B. Zonal Marking: Centre Back stays in line to provide cover and balance

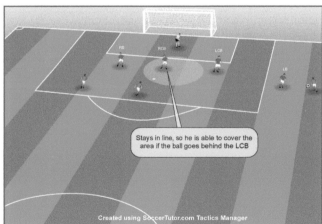

PRACTICE EXAMPLES FOR THE DEFENSIVE PHASE

1. Pressing to Win the Ball High Up the Pitch in a Dynamic 6 v 7 (+GK) Game

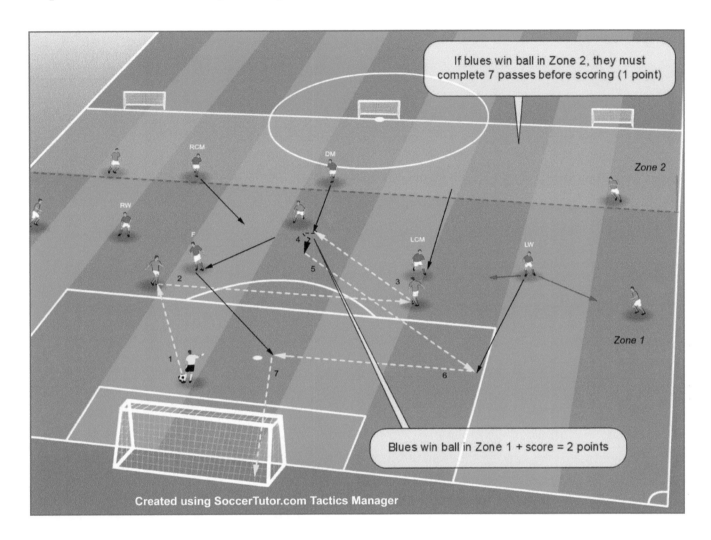

If blues win ball in Zone 2, they must complete 7 passes before scoring (1 point)

Blues win ball in Zone 1 + score = 2 points

Created using SoccerTutor.com Tactics Manager

Practice Description

Using half a full pitch, we mark out 2 zones as shown. There is a big goal with a goalkeeper at one end and 3 mini goals at the other end. We play 6 v 7 (+GK).

The red team have their back 4 and 3 midfielders. The blue team have 3 central midfielders, 2 wingers and 1 forward. The players are free to move across both zones, but the blues aim to win the ball in zone 1.

1. The practice starts with the red team's goalkeeper and the reds try to build up play through the blue team's pressure and score in one of the 3 mini goals.

2. The blue team's objective is to press and win the ball high up the pitch (within zone 1) and then launch a fast break attack, trying to score within 5 seconds (2 points).

Once the blues win the ball, only the 4 red defenders are still active and able to defend their goal.

If the blues win the ball inside zone 2, they must then complete 7 passes before they are able to try and score a goal (1 point). This restriction motivates the players to win the ball high up within zone 1.

2. Pressing to Win the Ball High Up the Pitch in a Dynamic 10 v 10 (+GK) Game

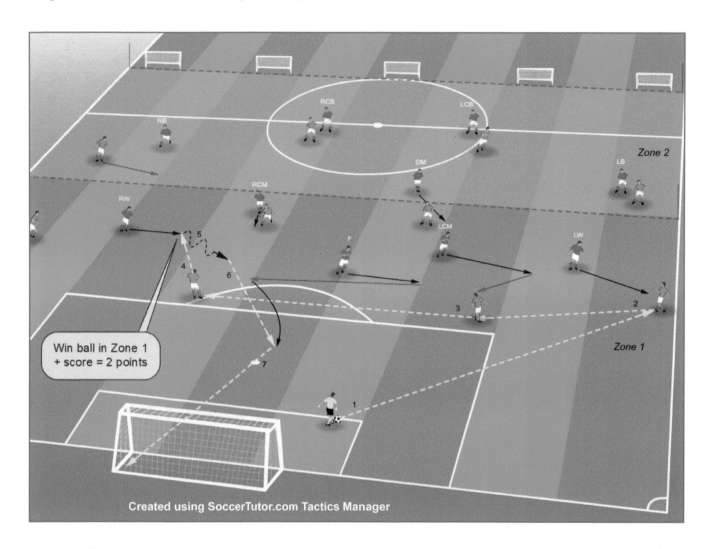

Win ball in Zone 1 + score = 2 points

Practice Description

This is a progression of the previous practice. We extend the size of the area and now play with all 20 outfield players.

The red team are in a 4-4-2 formation but you can change this to that of your next opponents.

The rules and objectives remain the same, however it is now even easier for the red team to score as there are 5 mini goals to aim at. This puts even more emphasis on the blues to win the ball high up the pitch and within zone 1.

3. Defensive Compactness and Quickly Getting Numbers Around the Ball in a Dynamic Game

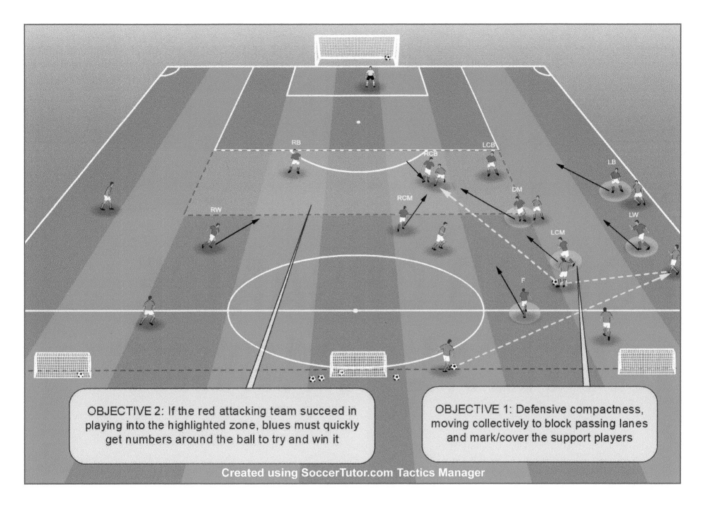

OBJECTIVE 2: If the red attacking team succeed in playing into the highlighted zone, blues must quickly get numbers around the ball to try and win it

OBJECTIVE 1: Defensive compactness, moving collectively to block passing lanes and mark/cover the support players

Created using SoccerTutor.com Tactics Manager

Objective 1 (Compacting Phase): Defending within your own half and keeping close distances to each other to stop the opposition playing between or through the lines.

Objective 2 (Prevention Phase): If the opposition do play in between the lines, react quickly to get numbers around the ball, limiting time and space to try to win it.

Practice Description

1. The reds are in the formation of the next opponents and the blues are in our 4-3-3 formation. The practice starts with the red team trying to play through the blue team's defensive organisation and then score past the goalkeeper.

2. The blue team initially use defensive compactness to try and prevent the reds from progressing their attack. If they win the ball, they try to score in one of the mini goals.

3. If the red attacking team are able to play through the blue's defensive compactness and into the highlighted area, the blues then change their objective to quickly get numbers around the ball to try and win it as soon as possible.

* See full tactical analysis on pages 162 and 163 for more information on "Compacting Phase: Keeping Short Distances Between Players and Lines" and "Prevention Phase: Limiting Time and Space Around the Ball."

CHAPTER 7

HOW TO ORGANISE TACTICAL TRAINING

THE TRAINING PROCESS

PRINCIPLES TO FOLLOW

1. REPETITION

The fundamental principle to follow, in order to learn and optimise technical and tactical competency (individual and collective), is "repetition."

Dimensions of the available space and the number of players involved in the training carried out affect the frequency and conditions for the repetition of the exercises being considered.

2. TRAINING CONDITIONS CLOSE TO COMPETITIVE MATCHES

The second important principle is the correlation of the training session to what we see on the pitch during competitive matches. A close connection between training practices and competitive matches favours the most effective response from our players and the best performances.

3. CORRECT DIFFICULTY LEVEL

The third important principle is making sure the difficulty of the training sessions matches up with the competence of the players. On this basis, practices that are too easy or too complicated can lead to flat results.

4. PROGRESSION

The fourth principle to follow is the progression of the work. If the session starts from basic concepts, it is then of fundamental importance to proceed gradually, adding more detailed concepts as you go. The players adapt and learn best this way.

PARAMETERS TO MANAGE

Parameters that are possible to change, in order to accelerate and optimise the learning process, are:

1. **Level of difficulty**

2. **Environment**

3. **Enjoyment of the process**

To increase the difficulty level, these aspects can be changed:

- The variables to be evaluated by the player (evaluation to be done in relation to the complexities of the tactical situation)

- The execution time/duration of the practice (evaluation to be based on the needs of the team/players)

- The presence or absence of an opponent

- The pressure (intensity) of the competition

In practical terms, to increase the difficulty level, one can, for example, increase or decrease the playing area, add active opponents or increase the number of balls to play with.

A good training practice/session impacts the participation level in a positive way and, indirectly, on absorbing new concepts (learning process).

Another parameter which influences the learning process is the surroundings. These include:

- Structures

- Weather conditions

- Interactions (even psychological) among the individual players and within the group

THE LEARNING PROCESS

Keeping in mind the principles and parameters mentioned so far, the coach must evaluate the level of the players and the team as a group, and proceed with accuracy.

A good progressive training session could anticipate the following practices:

- **Learning Practices** (without pressure)
- **Optimisation Practices** (pressure below standard of a competitive match)
- **Standard Practices** (level of difficulty comparable to a competitive match situation)
- **High Intensity Practices** (level of difficulty greater than a competitive match)

TRAINING ASPECTS FOR THE DIFFERENT PHASES OF THE GAME

From a team standpoint, the aspects that the coach must consider for his weekly planning are as follows:

1. ATTACKING PHASE

1a) Processes of Play:

- **Organised Attack:** Advancing with the ball
  (restart and build up play from the back)

- **Organised Attack:** Preparation
  (creating phase and accelerating the attack)

- **Organised Attack:** Finishing Phase
  (final pass/assists and finishing)

- **Restarts:** Reorganisation and positioning

- **Restarts:** Counter attacks

1b) Set Plays:

- **Corner kicks**
- **Direct free kicks** (central)
- **Indirect free kicks** (central)
- **Direct free kicks from long distance** (central)
- **Wide free kicks**
- **Wide free kicks from long distance**
- **Throw-ins**
- **Free kicks within own half**
- **Throw-ins within own half**
- **Goal Kicks**

2. DEFENSIVE PHASE

2a) Processes of Play:

- **Organised Defence:** Aggressive response
  (press high up the pitch)

- **Organised Defence:** Compactness
  (compact lines and preventative marking)

- **Organised Defence:** Winning the ball
  (reactions of defensive line & individual players)

- **Reorganisation:** Aggressive (reactive pressing)

- **Reorganisation:** Withdraw (get behind ball)

1b) Set Plays:

- **Defensive Corner kicks**
- **Defensive Direct free kicks** (central)
- **Defensive Indirect free kicks** (central)
- **Defensive Direct free kicks from long distance** (central)
- **Defensive Wide free kicks**
- **Defensive Wide free kicks from long distance**
- **Defensive Throw-ins**
- **Defensive Free kicks within own half**
- **Defensive Throw-ins within own half**
- **Defensive Goal Kicks**

3. THE TRANSITION PHASES

From a practical standpoint, it is possible to work in an **"Associated"** approach (combining attacking and defensive moves) or with a **"Separate"** approach (training each aspect separately). An **"Associated Practice"** can work on the transition from defence to attack in the following ways:

- Aggressive attack in the attacking third, followed by losing the ball, recovering it, and then finally trying to score again (very quickly).

- Compact organisation in the middle third, win the ball and either launch a fast break attack or start a positional attack.

- Winning the ball in the defensive third, followed by a counter attack or a positional attack.

We can also work on the transition from attack to defence in the following ways:

- Positional attack, followed by loss of possession and defensive reorganisation.

- Positional preparation, followed by loss of possession and the need to reorganise.

- Advancing with the ball, followed by loss of possession and the need to defend a possible counter attack from the opposition.

TRAINING METHODS

TRAINING METHODS

From a technical perspective, the training methods will have to develop not only the collective organisation and the aspects mentioned earlier, but also the individual technical skills and the communication amongst players in small areas or specific zones of the pitch.

The technical skill of an individual player, both in and out of possession, are the added value that enables a well organised team to improve their potential and the effectiveness of its movements.

On the contrary, individuals who are technically very skilled, but unable to cooperate with teammates inside a well organised tactical plan, will never be able to express their potential well, and this clearly affects the whole team negatively.

I. TECHNICAL TRAINING PRACTICES

TECHNICAL SEQUENCES

Through technical sequences, we stimulate the individual technical competency of the individual.

It's possible to work on one skill or on several skills, one after another (complex sequences). The coach works on improving the quality of the move, rather than the speed of execution.

TACTICAL SEQUENCES

The tactical sequences try to combine the accuracy of the technical skill with the speed of execution. And for this reason, 2 or more teams compete to execute the technical circuit in the minimum possible time.

RONDOS

Rondos are typically technical practices where we practice one-touch passing, receiving with the correct body shape, precision and speed of execution, all under individual defensive pressure.

Rondos represent an ideal way to start a training session, especially with elite teams, and have value in strengthening bonds within a group.

CONFRONTATION GAMES

The group is divided into 2 teams that execute 2 different technical-tactical sequences and confront each other, indirectly, in 2 or 3 efforts.

One team works on the time to complete the practice, while the other tries to pile up as many points as possible before the roles are reversed.

"1 v 1" DUELS

The players are grouped in teams, but carry out the practice as duels (1 v 1) and try to improve their performance levels under pressure from their direct opponent.

2. PATTERNS OF PLAY, POSSESSION GAMES AND SMALL SIDED GAMES

TACTICAL PATTERNS OF PLAY

In the attacking phase, throughout the playing sequences, the objective is to train the movements of the ball without the presence of the opponents. This is done by breaking down the complexity of the system of play into smaller parts (represented by one or more geometrical figures, such as rhombuses and triangles).

Patterns of play stimulate both the technical-tactical skills of the players and the communication/interaction amongst the players, recreating some typical situations in the processes of ball possession and preparation for accelerating the attack.

In the defensive phase, the objective is obviously different, but the structure of the practice is not greatly modified. Even in this case, the scope remains the collaboration within the group and simulating some typical situations that the players must learn how to face in the best way.

ATTACKING COMBINATION PLAY

Through combined actions, the objective is to train the attacking process, breaking down the module into geometrical figures (triangles/rhombuses) that now function as "dynamic platforms," which are useful to support the communication amongst players and the developments of the action.

Even with this type of practice, we can stimulate the technical-tactical competency of the players and collaborations amongst the players themselves.

POSSESSION GAMES

Even these types of practices are based on the usefulness of breaking down the playing module as a whole, into geometrical shapes. Individual competency and game organisation can then be trained inside of these shapes.

Ball possession practices train game situations thanks to the presence of opponents, the interaction amongst the players inside of typical geometrical

shapes and competency related to positioning, receiving with the correct body shape and passing.

Even in the defensive phase, players must collaborate, optimise their positioning, time their pressing movements and win the ball.

Utilising a limited number of players increases the frequency of participation for each individual player. This impacts the players in a positive way for the technical aspect, and creates the need for a high level of concentration for each individual player as well.

SMALL SIDED GAMES

Small sided games involve a reduced number of players and have appropriate modified rules. Having a lower number of players than in a regular match facilitates the intensity of the game and demands continuous participation of all individual players, increasing the possibility of learning and increasing tactical competency in the game situations included.

3. TACTICAL TRAINING PRACTICES

FUNCTIONAL PRACTICES

Functional practices are a way of training the whole team together, simulating the presence of opponents or with partially active opponents.

The objective is to learn and refine the collective movements in a simplified situation.

Varying the objectives inside of these type of practices makes it possible to find practices that can be employed in both the attacking and defensive phases.

POSITIONAL GAMES

Positional games represent a refinement of possession games. We focus on forming the triangle and rhombus shapes that are identical to those formed in the course of a competitive match. In positional games, the team, or part of it, is lined up according to our usual formation.

From a technical and organisational perspective, positional games are situational practices that very closely reproduce the problems seen in competitive matches on a full pitch and stimulate passing and receiving, while being fully contested by the opposition.

Positional games mainly train the possession phase, but also stimulate some defensive aspects, such as pressing and winning the ball.

POSITIONAL DEVELOPMENT PRACTICES

The structure of the practices is similar to that of positional games.

However, whereas positional games have the main objective of working on maintaining possession of the ball inside of triangle and rhombus shapes, positional development practices have the main objective of training the players to develop the ability of switching from the creating phase (creating an opening) to accelerating the attack.

TACTICAL PRACTICES

When it's necessary to train aspects or movements highly specific to a tactical situation from a competitive match, it is important to utilise practices that reproduce the exact game situations that we face, especially when regarding space and time.

In particular, repetitions of any situation create a natural adaptation on the part of the players involved.

These practices can of course be used to train both defensive and attacking aspects of the game.

GAMES WITH A THEME (TACTICAL)

Games with a theme are a valid way to direct the attention to specific situations with the whole team taking part.

By utilising restrictions, such as dividing the pitch into positional zones, it is possible to train some specific aspects, even with the whole team taking part.

Using games with a theme, it is possible to train both the attacking and defensive phases.

ORGANISING TRAINING SESSIONS

ORGANISING TRAINING SESSIONS

We recommend that the training session include "connected material."

Consequently, it is appropriate that the various practices be connected. There should be a logical order, starting with a technical practice which uses the technical skills to be required for the following practices in the session. This practice should also be in line with the principal objective.

However, it's also possible to work in a disjointed fashion. In this case, the sequence of the work is not working on the same themes, but the initial practices in the session are introductory to meet objectives that will be achieved in future sessions.

In general, it's useful to divide the session into 3 or 4 phases:

- **1st PHASE:** Technical Practice
- **2nd PHASE:** Practice for maintaining possession or specific situational practices
- **3rd PHASE:** Tactical Practice
- **4th PHASE:** Game or Game with a Theme

Of course, the above indications for how to plan a session are general and unspecific. The coach will have to adapt the objectives and the work weekly, related to the needs of the team.

Naturally, significant adjustments need to be made for teams that have lower numbers of sessions per week.

Throughout the technical practices, we concentrate our attention on the development of individual skills (player's technical actions within specific space).

In the second phase, we develop individual competency and the communication amongst players to resolve restricted (in terms of space) game situations. The third and eventually the fourth phase of the session are dedicated to the team and the tactical organisation of the whole team.

In particular, in the third and fourth phases, the objectives refer to the following aspects:

ORGANISED ATTACK

1. Build Up Play from the Back
2. Build Up Play from the Back, followed by defensive transition (reorganisation)
3. Creating Phase + Accelerating the Attack
4. Attacking against different formations (positional play), followed by defensive transition (reorganisation)
5. Finishing Phase
6. Finishing Phase, followed by defensive transition (the need to stop/control possible counter attacks)

REGAINING POSSESSION

7. Positional attack
   (accelerating the attack and finishing phase)
8. Counter attacks

ORGANISED DEFENCE

9. Pressing the ball carrier
10. Pressing the ball carrier in the high zone, winning the ball and fast break attack
11. Compactness
    (close spaces and preventative marking)
12. Compactness in middle zone, followed by winning the ball and positional attack
13. Winning the ball
    (collective reactions of the defensive line and reactions of individual defenders)
14. Winning the ball in the low zone, followed by a positional attack or counter attack

REORGANISATION

15. Aggressive pressing (reactive)
16. Withdraw (get behind the ball)

TRAINING WEEK EXAMPLE (5 SESSIONS)

MONDAY

Rest.

TUESDAY

Traditionally, after playing a competitive match on Sunday, we have a rest day on Monday and training restarts on Tuesday. This includes an evaluation of the players' physical status and analysis of the previous match, pointing out positive aspects and aspects that need to be improved.

The Tuesday training session focuses on physical (athletic) work and on practices related to difficulties encountered in the previous game.

WEDNESDAY

On Wednesday, after the usual technical practice, the team works on the attacking and defensive phases. The tactical work centres on training the defensive sector and the attacking developments in the attacking third. If we know the characteristics of our next opponent, the work just mentioned is carried out in relation to those characteristics.

We play a game with a theme at the end which includes elements that train midfielders and forwards on how to develop the play in the attacking third and how to proceed for restarting an attack after losing the ball. We also work on the related effort of our defensive block to recover the ball and then play forward.

THURSDAY

In Thursday's session, we work on positional play that is useful to train ball circulation and the reactions for both transition phases.

The tactical training focuses on attacking positional play (creating phase) and defensive compactness in the middle zone.

The game with a theme focuses on restarting play from goal kicks, build up play from the back and accelerating coordinated attacks using the defenders and midfielders.

The opposition in this training session include forwards and midfielders (organised according to the formation of our next opponent), who will try to recover the ball and then score themselves.

FRIDAY

The Friday session includes the usual technical warm-up, followed by a positional play practice.

From a tactical standpoint, the central practice has the team attacking forcefully in the attacking third (high zone) and in the middle third, in order to win the ball and launch a fast break attack. This is done with the idea of training the best developments that we can use to create difficulties for our next opponents.

The game with a theme, instead, includes elements that train build up play and defensive compactness, providing different scenarios to the teams when the ball is recovered.

On one side, there is a group that will have to work on maintaining possession as soon as the ball is recovered, whereas the other group will look to launch fast counter attacks.

SATURDAY

Saturday's session includes rehearsal-style training for the finishing phase, alongside the final reminder to the players of the strategic points for the match the following day.

SUNDAY

Match Day.

CHAPTER 8

TRAINING SESSION EXAMPLES

TRAINING SESSIONS: THE FUNDAMENTALS FROM THE WORLD'S TOP COACHES

The work on the training pitch is extremely important.

The players are the stars during the match but during the coaching session, the role of the coach is fundamental and he is more important than the players.

The coach must prepare every sessions and pay attention during the work on the pitch.

In my career I had the opportunity to follow the full training week (coaching sessions) of some of the best coaches in the world like **Marcello Lippi**, **Carlo Ancelotti**, **Pep Guardiola**, **Maurizio Sarri**, **Diego Simeone**, **Luciano Spalletti**, **Luis Enrique** and many others.

These are the fundamental things that I have learned during this time:

- Top coaches use only a few training practices in a session, but they are very well managed by the coach.

- Repetition is fundamental to improve the connections between the players so it's much better to follow the same work, instead of changing the practices every week.

- The coach must know, in every detail, the right training practices for his game model. If you know a lot of practices but you are not able to manage the details sufficiently, it is impossible to be efficient.

- To be efficient during the training sessions, it is also very important to know the objectives and the objectives depends on the level and the age of the players.

- Other aspects, such as the weather, the time of year and more have to be assessed, as they can influence the training session.

In the following pages, I have presented some training session examples.

I like to start with a rondo (after a warm up if it is necessary) and then continue with a possession practice with the players in their specific tactical positions, even if the area is small.

After this first part of the training session (maximum of 25 minutes), I use tactical practices to develop a specific phase of the game (attacking phase, defensive phase or transition phases).

I like to start without real opposition (tactical pattern with passive or partial pressure) and then finish with a fully competitive tactical game.

We have no more than 4 practices in a training session.

In the examples to follow, the first training session focuses on build up play and the second focuses on positional attacks.

TRAINING SESSION EXAMPLE 1 (BUILD UP PLAY)

I. 5 v 2 Positional Rondo Possession Game

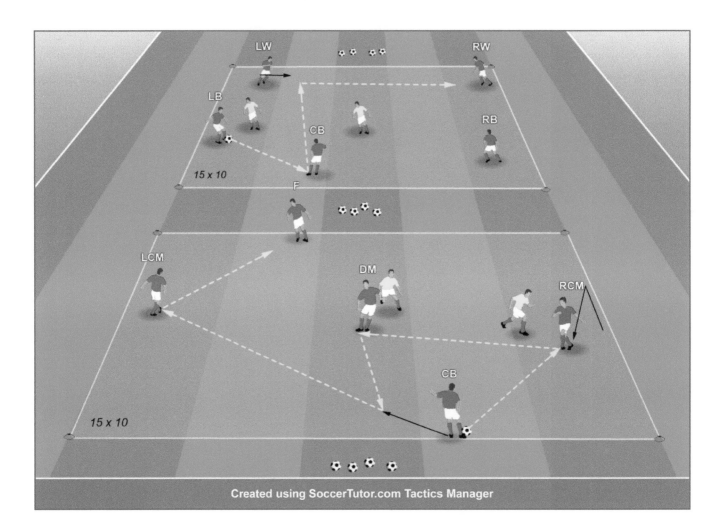

Created using SoccerTutor.com Tactics Manager

Objective: Passing, receiving, maintaining possessions - technical tools for building up play.

Practice Description

We mark out two 15 x 10 metre/yard areas and play simple 5 v 2 rondo possession games.

The blue players are in their specific tactical roles:

- **TOP RONDO:** CB at base, LB, RB, LW and RW at sides.
- **BOTTOM RONDO:** CB at base, LCM and RCM at sides, Forward (F) at top and DM in the middle.

The 2 yellow players try to recover the ball, while the 5 blue players aim to keep possession of the ball.

Increase the intensity progressively throughout.

2. Positional 10 v 10 Possession Game

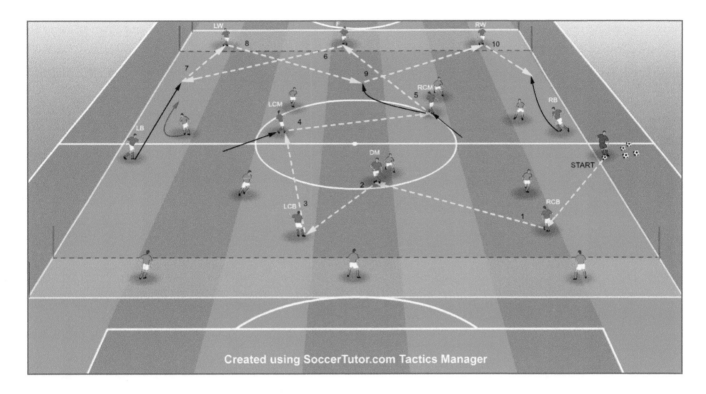

Created using SoccerTutor.com Tactics Manager

Objective: Ball circulation and possession play (passing, receiving, movement) to practice build up play.

Practice Description

We divide the area into 1 main zone and 2 smaller end zones. In the main zone, both teams have their back 4, 1 defensive midfielder and 2 central midfielders. In the end zones, the teams have 2 wingers and 1 forward. All players must stay within their respective zones throughout.

The practice starts with the coach's pass and that team (blues in diagram) try to complete 10 consecutive passes with help from the 3 players in the end zone, who have to move effectively and use the correct body shape to receive their teammates passes.

If the defending team (reds in diagram) win the ball, the team roles are reversed and the practice continues. The reds then try to complete 10 passes and the blues try to recover the ball.

Make sure to allow for sufficient rest periods during this practice. This practice is quite intense, especially for the defending team that has to be constantly pressing in order to try and win the ball.

3. Tactical Build Up Pattern of Play

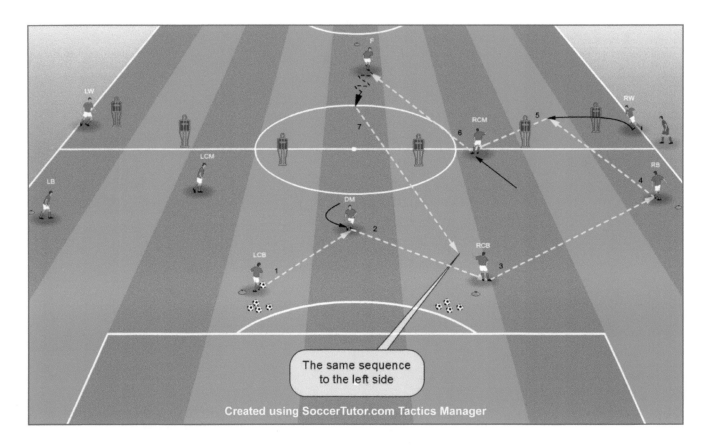

The same sequence to the left side

Created using SoccerTutor.com Tactics Manager

Objective: Tactical pattern to build up play from the back, including an "Imbucata" pass through the midfield line.

Practice Description

Using a full pitch, we have 9 players in their specific positions within the 4-3-3 formation (back 4, 1 defensive midfielder, 2 central midfielders, 2 wingers and 1 forward). We also have 6 mannequins which represent the opponents.

1. The left centre back (LCB) starts the practice with a pass to the defensive midfielder (DM).

2. The DM passes to the other centre back (RCB).

3. RCB passes to the right back (RB).

4. The right back (RB) plays a strong forward pass to the winger (RW), who moves inside to receive.

5. The winger (RW) lays the ball back to the oncoming central midfielder (RCM).

6. RCM passes to the forward (F).

7. The forward takes a touch back and passes the ball back to the start position.

The same sequence starts again immediately towards the other side with RCB's pass to the DM.

* You can use this practice to work on various different patterns - see tactical analysis in Chapters 2 and 3.

4. Build Up Play from the Back to Finish in a Dynamic Tactical Game

Created using SoccerTutor.com Tactics Manager

Objective: Building up play from the back (playing through pressure).

Practice Description

The blues use a 4-3-3 formation and the reds are in the formation of our next opponents.

1. The practice starts from the goalkeeper and one of the centre backs can drop into the first zone to collect a free pass. From here, the blue team build up play, trying to evade the pressure from the red team.

2. The blues try to move the ball into third the zone where there is initially a 3 v 4 numerical disadvantage. However, 1 player can move forward (LCM in diagram) to create an equality of numbers

3. Once in the third zone, the blues try to score (1 point).

4. If the red team win the ball at any time, their aim is to launch a fast break attack to score as quickly as possible (1 point). If they score within 6-8 seconds, they score 2 points.

5. The blue team make a fast transition from attack to defence. If they recover the ball, they score 1 point.

6. If the ball goes out of play at any time, restart from the blue team's goalkeeper.

TRAINING SESSION EXAMPLE 2 (POSITIONAL ATTACKS)

I. 3 Team Rondo Possession Game

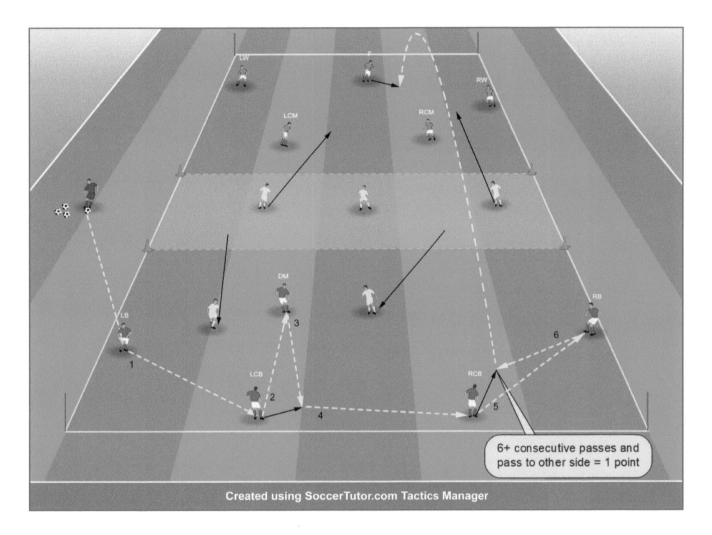

6+ consecutive passes and
pass to other side = 1 point

Created using SoccerTutor.com Tactics Manager

Practice Description

Set up two 15 x 10 metre/yard end zones and 1 smaller 15 x 5 metre/yard zone in between them. We have 3 teams, each with 5, 6 or 7 players. In this example, each team has 5 players.

1. The practice starts with the coach's pass into the first zone and the blue team try to maintain possession against 2 yellow opponents who move from the middle zone.

2. The blue team's aim is to complete 6 consecutive passes and then play an aerial pass to the red team (over the middle zone) in the opposite zone to score 1 point.

3. Two yellow players move from the middle zone to contest the red team and the other 2 move into the middle zone. We have the same situation with the same objectives in the far zone, now with 5 reds against 2 yellow players.

4. If the yellows win the ball, 2 blue players move across to contest the reds and the other 3 blue players move into the middle zone. All 5 yellow players move to the opposite zone, ready to receive an aerial pass from the reds.

The team that is able to complete 6 passes and successfully play to the team in the opposite zone the most amount of times wins the game.

2. Checking Away from Marker and Playing Forward in a Diamond Passing Drill

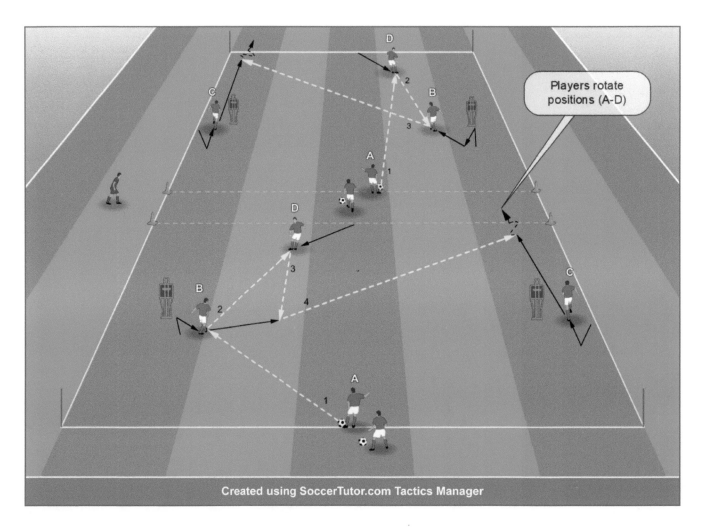

Players rotate positions (A-D)

Created using SoccerTutor.com Tactics Manager

Objective: Technical skills - passing, checking away from marker before moving to receive and quick combination play to practice positional attacks and playing in behind.

Practice Description

In the same 15 x 25 metre/yard total area, we have 2 groups of 5 players working simultaneously. 4 players (A, B, C & D) are positioned in a diamond and there are 2 mannequins which represent opponents.

The players execute different combinations in both zones. Here is one combination (bottom of diagram):

1. A passes to B, who checks away from the mannequin (opponent) before moving to receive.

2. B passes forward to D (one touch) and moves inside to receive the ball back.

3. D passes back to B.

4. C checks away from the mannequin (opponent) and makes a forward run. B passes for C to run onto and control.

5. The players move to the next position (A-> B -> C -> D -> A) and the sequence starts again with the next player waiting.

3. Creating an Opening and Passing in Behind in a Dynamic 4 Zone Game

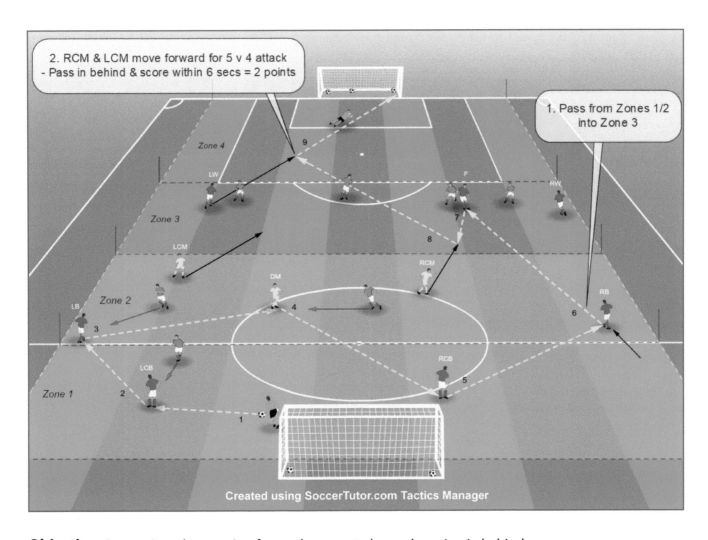

2. RCM & LCM move forward for 5 v 4 attack
- Pass in behind & score within 6 secs = 2 points

1. Pass from Zones 1/2 into Zone 3

Created using SoccerTutor.com Tactics Manager

Objective: Possession play, passing forward, support play and passing in behind.

Practice Description

We mark out 4 zones as shown with 2 teams of 7 players + 2 GKs and 3 neutral players (DM, LCM & RCM).

1. The goalkeeper starts and the blues have a 7 v 3 advantage across Zones 1 and 2 with help from the yellow neutral players. The aim is to create an opening for a blue player to pass to a teammate in Zone 3.

2. Once a player receives in space (RB in diagram) and there is an opening, he passes forward to a teammate in Zone 2. The yellow LCM and RCM can then both move forward into Zone 3.

3. The aim is to play in behind as quickly as possible and score (within 6 seconds = 2 points). The reds must stay within Zone 3.

4. When a phase is finished, restart with the red team's goalkeeper and the team roles reversed.

If the defending team (reds) win the ball at any time, they then launch a fast break attack to try and score.

4. Creating an Opening and Passing in Behind in a 10 v 7 (+GK) Positional Game

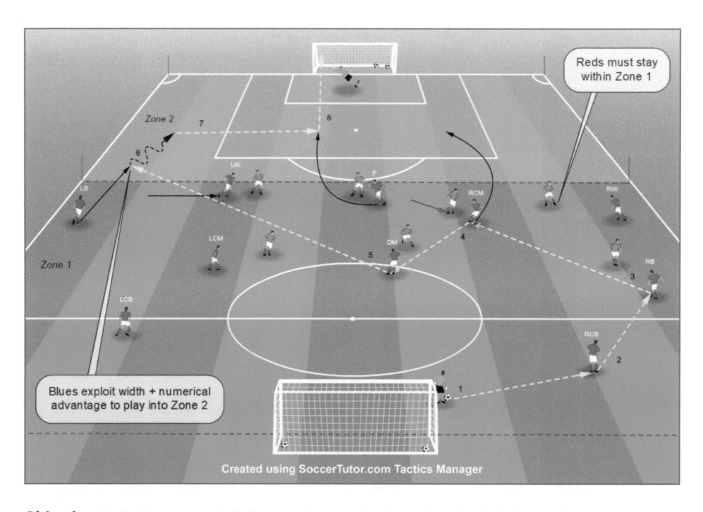

Objective: Exploiting a numerical advantage in a positional attack to play in behind and score.

Practice Description

We have a full blue team against 7 red outfield players (4-3 formation) + GK.

1. The practice starts with the blue attacking team as they try to take advantage of their numerical superiority to build up play and create an opening. In particular, they can exploit the space out wide.

2. The main aim is to play the ball in behind into Zone 2. From there, the blues finish the attack. The reds are not allowed to move into Zone 2 to defend.

3. The red defending team keep compact, defend and try to win the ball. If the reds do win the ball, they then launch a counter attack and try to score.

4. When an attack is finished or the ball goes out of play, restart from the blue goalkeeper.

* The blues can practice many different build up and attacking combinations to achieve their objective of playing in behind. You can use the different tactical examples shown in the tactical analysis of this book.

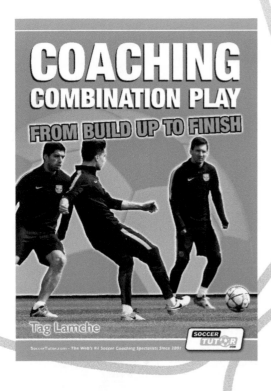

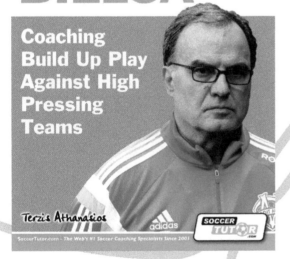
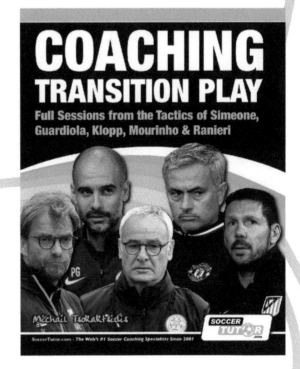

CPSIA information can be obtained
at www.ICGtesting.com
Printed in the USA
BVHW021632010819
554776BV00013B/119/P